JULIUS ERVING

JULIUS ERVING

❦

Josh Wilker

CHELSEA HOUSE PUBLISHERS
New York Philadelphia

Dedication: For my brother, Ian.

Chelsea House Publishers
Editorial Director Richard Rennert
Executive Managing Editor Karyn Gullen Browne
Copy Chief Robin James
Picture Editor Adrian G. Allen
Art Director Robert Mitchell
Manufacturing Director Gerald Levine
Assistant Art Director Joan Ferrigno

Black Americans of Achievement
Senior Editor Philip Koslow

Staff for JULIUS ERVING
Editorial Assistant Sydra Mallery
Assistant Designer John Infantino
Picture Researcher Alan Gottlieb
Cover Illustrator Richard Leonard

First Printing

1 3 5 7 9 8 6 4 2

Library of Congress Cataloging-in-Publication Data
Wilker, Josh.
    Julius Erving / Josh Wilker.
    p. cm. — (Black Americans of achievement)
    Includes bibliographical references and index.
    ISBN 0-7910-1125-9
       0-7910-1150-X (pbk.)
    1. Erving, Julius—Juvenile literature. 2. Basketball players—
United States—Biography—Juvenile literature. [1. Erving, Julius.
2.Basketball players. 3.Afro-Americans—Biography.] I.Title.
II.Series.
GV884.E89W55 1995   94–13206
796.323'092—dc20   CIP
[B]   AC

Frontispiece: *Julius Erving goes up
for a dunk against the San Antonio
Spurs on October 22, 1976.*

CONTENTS

BLACK AMERICANS OF ACHIEVEMENT

HENRY AARON
baseball great

KAREEM ABDUL-JABBAR
basketball great

RALPH ABERNATHY
civil rights leader

ALVIN AILEY
choreographer

MUHAMMAD ALI
heavyweight champion

RICHARD ALLEN
*religious leader and
social activist*

MAYA ANGELOU
author

LOUIS ARMSTRONG
musician

ARTHUR ASHE
tennis great

JOSEPHINE BAKER
entertainer

JAMES BALDWIN
author

BENJAMIN BANNEKER
scientist and mathematician

AMIRI BARAKA
poet and playwright

COUNT BASIE
bandleader and composer

ROMARE BEARDEN
artist

JAMES BECKWOURTH
frontiersman

MARY MCLEOD BETHUNE
educator

JULIAN BOND
civil rights leader and politician

GWENDOLYN BROOKS
poet

JIM BROWN
football great

RALPH BUNCHE
diplomat

STOKELY CARMICHAEL
civil rights leader

GEORGE WASHINGTON
CARVER
botanist

RAY CHARLES
musician

CHARLES CHESNUTT
author

JOHN COLTRANE
musician

BILL COSBY
entertainer

PAUL CUFFE
merchant and abolitionist

COUNTEE CULLEN
poet

BENJAMIN DAVIS, SR., AND
BENJAMIN DAVIS, JR.
military leaders

SAMMY DAVIS, JR.
entertainer

FATHER DIVINE
religious leader

FREDERICK DOUGLASS
abolitionist editor

CHARLES DREW
physician

W. E. B. DU BOIS
scholar and activist

PAUL LAURENCE DUNBAR
poet

KATHERINE DUNHAM
dancer and choreographer

DUKE ELLINGTON
bandleader and composer

RALPH ELLISON
author

JULIUS ERVING
basketball great

JAMES FARMER
civil rights leader

ELLA FITZGERALD
singer

MARCUS GARVEY
black nationalist leader

JOSH GIBSON
baseball great

DIZZY GILLESPIE
musician

WHOOPI GOLDBERG
entertainer

ALEX HALEY
author

PRINCE HALL
social reformer

MATTHEW HENSON
explorer

CHESTER HIMES
author

BILLIE HOLIDAY
singer

LENA HORNE
entertainer

LANGSTON HUGHES
poet

ZORA NEALE HURSTON
author

JESSE JACKSON
civil rights leader and politician

MICHAEL JACKSON
entertainer

JACK JOHNSON
heavyweight champion

JAMES WELDON JOHNSON
author

MAGIC JOHNSON
basketball great

SCOTT JOPLIN
composer

BARBARA JORDAN
politician

MICHAEL JORDAN
basketball great

CORETTA SCOTT KING
civil rights leader

MARTIN LUTHER KING, JR.
civil rights leader

LEWIS LATIMER
scientist

SPIKE LEE
filmmaker

CARL LEWIS
champion athlete

JOE LOUIS
heavyweight champion

RONALD MCNAIR
astronaut

MALCOLM X
militant black leader

THURGOOD MARSHALL
Supreme Court justice

TONI MORRISON
author

ELIJAH MUHAMMAD
religious leader

EDDIE MURPHY
entertainer

JESSE OWENS
champion athlete

SATCHEL PAIGE
baseball great

CHARLIE PARKER
musician

GORDON PARKS
photographer

ROSA PARKS
civil rights leader

SIDNEY POITIER
actor

ADAM CLAYTON
POWELL, JR.
political leader

COLIN POWELL
military leader

LEONTYNE PRICE
opera singer

A. PHILIP RANDOLPH
labor leader

PAUL ROBESON
singer and actor

JACKIE ROBINSON
baseball great

DIANA ROSS
entertainer

BILL RUSSELL
basketball great

JOHN RUSSWURM
publisher

SOJOURNER TRUTH
antislavery activist

HARRIET TUBMAN
antislavery activist

NAT TURNER
slave revolt leader

DENMARK VESEY
slave revolt leader

ALICE WALKER
author

MADAM C. J. WALKER
entrepreneur

BOOKER T. WASHINGTON
educator and racial spokesman

IDA WELLS-BARNETT
civil rights leader

WALTER WHITE
civil rights leader

OPRAH WINFREY
entertainer

STEVIE WONDER
musician

RICHARD WRIGHT
author

ON ACHIEVEMENT

——— ❧ ———

Coretta Scott King

BEFORE YOU BEGIN this book, I hope you will ask yourself what the word *excellence* means to you. I think that it's a question we should all ask, and keep asking as we grow older and change. Because the truest answer to it should never change. When you think of excellence, perhaps you think of success at work; or of becoming wealthy; or meeting the right person, getting married, and having a good family life.

Those important goals are worth striving for, but there is a better way to look at excellence. As Martin Luther King, Jr., said in one of his last sermons, "I want you to be first in love. I want you to be first in moral excellence. I want you to be first in generosity. If you want to be important, wonderful. If you want to be great, wonderful. But recognize that he who is greatest among you shall be your servant."

My husband, Martin Luther King, Jr., knew that the true meaning of achievement is service. When I met him, in 1952, he was already ordained as a Baptist preacher and was working toward a doctoral degree at Boston University. I was studying at the New England Conservatory and dreamed of accomplishments in music. We married a year later, and after I graduated the following year we moved to Montgomery, Alabama. We didn't know it then, but our notions of achievement were about to undergo a dramatic change.

You may have read or heard about what happened next. What began with the boycott of a local bus line grew into a national movement, and by the time he was assassinated in 1968 my husband had fashioned a black movement powerful enough to shatter forever the practice of racial segregation. What you may not have read about is where he got his method for resisting injustice without compromising his religious beliefs.

He adopted the strategy of nonviolence from a man of a different race, who lived in a different country, and even practiced a different religion. The man was Mahatma Gandhi, the great leader of India, who devoted his life to serving humanity in the spirit of love and nonviolence. It was in these principles that Martin discovered his method for social reform. More than anything else, those two principles were the key to his achievements.

This book is about black Americans who served society through the excellence of their achievements. It forms a part of the rich history of black men and women in America—a history of stunning accomplishments in every field of human endeavor, from literature and art to science, industry, education, diplomacy, athletics, jurisprudence, even polar exploration.

Not all of the people in this history had the same ideals, but I think you will find something that all of them had in common. Like Martin Luther King, Jr., they all decided to become "drum majors" and serve humanity. In that principle—whether it was expressed in books, inventions, or song—they found something outside themselves to use as a goal and a guide. Something that showed them a way to serve others, instead of only living for themselves.

Reading the stories of these courageous men and women not only helps us discover the principles that we will use to guide our own lives but also teaches us about our black heritage and about America itself. It is crucial for us to know the heroes and heroines of our history and to realize that the price we paid in our struggle for equality in America was dear. But we must also understand that we have gotten as far as we have partly because America's democratic system and ideals made it possible.

We are still struggling with racism and prejudice. But the great men and women in this series are a tribute to the spirit of our democratic ideals and the system in which they have flourished. And that makes their stories special and worth knowing. ◆

1

"JUST CALL ME DOCTOR"

THE NEW KID snared the careening rebound one-handed and was gone. He piston-dribbled end to end past all but two reeling defenders, and those he turned to slack-jawed statues when he rocketed up into the sky. In the packed courtside bleachers children hollered, women laughed, and grown men rocked and squealed like newborns. The college kid with the enormous hands was showing them things they had never seen.

These were the Rucker League fans of Harlem: for years they had watched the best summertime basketball in the world. They had seen Hall of Famers like Wilt Chamberlain, Willis Reed, and Kareem Abdul-Jabbar face off against playground legends known as the Helicopter, Jumping Jackie, and the Goat.

"The most exciting play I've ever seen," according to Abdul-Jabbar, the National Basketball Association (NBA) lifetime leader in games played, happened in a Rucker game: Chamberlain turned and fired his famous fall-away jumper, and the legendary Jumping Jackie skied to pin it on the backboard two and a half feet above the rim. By the summer of 1970, Rucker League fans had, like Abdul-Jabbar, seen their share of basketball acrobatics. Unlike those who watched the slower-paced NBA, Rucker League fans were connoisseurs of the astonishing. They did not come to the games to root for one team or another but to witness midair miracles.

Little could be done on a basketball court that would surprise them. But now there was a new legend

Whirling along the baseline, Dr. J drives to the hoop in a 1975 American Basketball Association (ABA) contest between the New York Nets and the Spirits of St. Louis. After Erving joined the ABA in 1971, his astonishing talent gave the new league instant credibility with the fans and the media.

in the making. The college kid from nowhere made them all feel like they had not seen anything yet. And no one even knew his name.

A man at the scorer's table was bellowing into a megaphone. "Little Hawk!" he boomed when the kid swooped down the lane for an elegant finger roll. "Black Moses!" he cried when the kid reverse-jammed. The names dissolved in the joyous roar of the crowd, but the megaphone man kept trying: "Houdini," "Magic," "The Claw." None of the nicknames fit. Some of them even seemed to irritate the kid. During a time-out, he made his way to the scorer's table.

Fans near the table hushed. Few had even heard the quiet kid speak. The megaphone man looked up to see that the young player who was dominating the game had scarcely broken a sweat. "Listen," the kid said in a quiet but deep and resonant voice. "Why don't you just call me Doctor."

Julius Erving's grade-school nickname was soon hailing down from every corner of the Rucker League bleachers. More and more fans flocked to his games, hoping to get a look at the newly anointed king of playground ball. One of Erving's Rucker League teammates recalled that when the Doctor arrived at the crowded court, "the mob would part like the waters of the Red Sea."

He had more moves than any of the NBA players. He had more moves than Helicopter, Jumping Jackie, or even the Goat. He poured in an average of 45 points a game. Some of his moves sparked screaming, shouting, foot-stomping explosions. At the end of one particularly raucous show—Erving would finish with 53 points—the Doctor made the whole neighborhood quake.

The move started out looking like a rare failure. To avoid the five defenders keying on him, the soaring Erving had to fly past the basket. Only the wildest of shots seemed possible as he sailed out of bounds. So Erving expanded the possibilities. He lashed out behind his head with his left hand and clamped onto the rim, snapping his body back around, and then with his free hand he clawed in a ferocious slam.

As the crowd exploded, the ball drilled the pavement and bounced straight up, back up through the chain net, up over the shivering rim—where it seemed to momentarily hover—before nestling feather-soft back down through the chain.

"The fence and trees began to shake," recalled Marty Bell in *The Legend of Dr. J.* "Confetti came down from the sixteenth floor." The cacophony Erving sparked kept up all summer long. By the final Rucker games, a Dr. J fan several blocks away could tell by the sound when a new move had just been unveiled.

In one of his last Rucker games, Erving got hemmed in by three defenders on the right baseline below the hoop. He had given up his dribble, and the towering three-man wall cut off all passing lanes. The only possible solution was flight.

"Sometimes when I start a play," Erving once said, "I never know if I will be able to do what I would like. But I always go ahead and try. I guess it's sort of like daring to be great." He floated out from under the basket, tossed the ball high off the backboard, whipped free in midair, and winged impossibly across the lane. The carom was wild. Erving climbed invisible stairs to gather it in. Then he whirled like a kite and slammed.

Before the announcer again bellowed his nickname into a megaphone, before the confetti came raining down, before the fans loosed another joyful shout, there was a moment, thinner than a heartbeat, when nobody even breathed. The backboard trembled. The Doctor touched down.

Young players in the Holcombe Rucker Community League pose with Harold S. Geneen of the ITT Corporation, one of the league's sponsors. In 1970, at the annual Rucker tournament for older players, 19-year-old Julius Erving first displayed his dazzling moves for Harlem's sophisticated basketball fans.

Three years later, it was Kevin Loughery's turn. Loughery thought he had seen everything. He had played against Oscar Robertson, Elgin Baylor, Jerry West, and Walt Frazier. He had started in the same backcourt as the magnificent Earl Monroe. Eleven years in the NBA had shown him basketball's best.

In 1973, he left the NBA to become a coach in the renegade American Basketball Association (ABA) and was immediately bombarded with lofty descriptions about the star player of his new team.

People told him Julius Erving could do things on a basketball court that no one else could do. Loughery replied, "Yeah, right." For many players and coaches in the NBA, Dr. J was a myth. Loughery did not believe in myths. He only believed what he saw.

"In the first game that I coached Doc with the Nets," Loughery recalled, "Doc drove the baseline and found himself under the basket with both George McGinnis and Darnell Hillman—two big guys— going for the block. Somehow, Doc floated between McGinnis and Hillman and then almost tore the rim down with a slam. To that point in my life, that was the greatest dunk I had ever seen, and Doc did it in the first half of my first game with him."

Erving had already impressed the playground experts at the Rucker games. When he joined the ABA in 1971, he quickly began to do the same to hardened basketball professionals like Kevin Loughery. Statements of reverence and awe followed him wherever he went. Players and coaches, who generally speak in only the most mundane clichés, often ended up sounding like frazzled UFO eyewitnesses.

"He took the whole building through the net," raved coach Bob Bass of the Miami Floridians after an Erving slam. "He took off into the stratosphere, then he dunked the ball with so much force that he created such a vacuum that everyone's ears cracked."

Other coaches, like San Diego's Stan Albeck, abandoned their well-ordered postgame rituals to chase down the Doctor like ecstatic children. "Man, I thought I'd seen everything," Albeck gushed as he hustled after Erving. "But that 360-degree job! Nobody's ever done anything like that! It was unbelievable!"

Loughery was also driven to strange behavior. In the latter stages of one of his team's victories, he called what seemed to be an unnecessary time-out. "I called that time-out," he explained directly to

Erving, "because I wanted to tell you that you've just played the greatest three-minute stretch of basketball I have ever seen."

In the eyes of his peers, Erving was in a league by himself.

Zelmo Beatty, a premiere player in the NBA for seven years before coming to the Doctor's league, believed Erving was carving out a special place for himself in history. "I saw Elgin Baylor in his prime and I saw Connie Hawkins," said Beatty, mentioning the two high-flying players that Erving was most often compared to. "No one could run and dunk and swoop down on the basket with the style of a young Julius Erving."

Billy Cunningham, who defended against Erving before becoming a coach in the NBA, extended Beatty's historical claim by comparing Erving favorably to a player who came after him, a man named Michael Jordan. Cunningham said, "Julius was the best player I've ever seen in the open court, and that includes Jordan."

Hubie Brown coached against both Jordan and Erving. After recounting an Erving dunk—"He had a move from the right side where he'd drive, raise up and take the ball in both hands, touch it against the top square over the rim, then slam it home"—Brown concluded that the Doctor "made plays no one has seen before or since, plays that not even Michael Jordan can do."

The former ABA star Steve "Snapper" Jones, who often watched Jordan from the sidelines as a television analyst, believes that of the two, "Julius played much higher above the rim." To Jones, Jordan and Erving stand alone at the pinnacle of the game as "players who have no limits."

"When a player as gifted as Julius takes the court," Jones said, "he believes he has no limitations." In his first few years in the pros, it seemed there was nothing

Erving launches a running hook in the lane during the ABA All-Star Game, played in Denver, Colorado, in 1976. During the 1975–76 season, Erving led the ABA in scoring with a 29.3 average.

Erving could not do. An ABA publicist once approached him before a game to tell him that there were only two players, Darrel Griffith and David Thompson, who could perform the 360-degree slam dunk. Erving looked at the basket, adjusted his knee brace, and scratched his chin. Then he bounded forward and took off. "Make that three," the Doctor said as the dunked ball skittered toward the sidelines.

McNichols Arena, in the mile-high city of Denver, Colorado, was packed with a capacity crowd of 15,021. When hometown player David Thompson threw down a 360-degree jam, the crowd went wild. "We're a mile high," began Maurice Lucas, an all-star watching from the sidelines. He motioned to Thompson, the young Denver Nuggets guard known as Skywalker, and hollered over the noise: "He's two miles high!"

It was halftime of the 1976 ABA All-Star Game, and David Thompson was challenging Dr. J for the title of most spectacular player in the world. The challenger strolled off the floor after his final dunk. The all-stars like Lucas watching the first ever slam-dunk contest from the sidelines weighed in with their expert judgments. "Oh no," Artis Gilmore of the Kentucky Colonels summed up, "Doc's in trouble."

It was clear, however, as soon as the 6-foot-6 inch, 200-pound Erving strode onto the empty court that he was in no trouble at all. Thompson may have been an outstanding leaper with a flair for the dramatic, but the Doctor was something more. "I'm like a jazzman," Erving had once said. "When it's my turn to solo, I'm not about to play the same old riff."

He started the thunderous music with a dunk he called the Iron Cross, flying in spread-eagle from the left and no-look slamming the ball behind his head. His second dunk was a rim-grabbing claw job reminiscent of the move that made Harlem shake. Then the Doctor grabbed two of the red-white-and-blue ABA balls, and from a standstill, his back to the basket, he elevated for an arena-rocking, twin-windmill double jam.

Though there was still one final dunk to come, Thompson already sensed he was beaten. The fans also knew that the man-to-man contest was over, but still they started screaming when Dr. J, standing at the foul line, a ball clenched in his right hand, turned his back to the basket and slowly paced all the way down to the other side of the court. He turned and faced the basket again. "There was silence," said Carl Scheer, general manager of the Denver Nuggets. "The crowd knew it was going to see something special."

In his first five years as a pro, Erving had attacked the basket from every angle. He had flown around, through, and over every defense concocted by opposing coaches. His imagination when playing ball seemed boundless. Once, an amazed teammate asked about a particularly astounding Dr. J dunk, and Erving replied, "Last night, I had a dream and I saw myself do it." Dreams became reality when Dr. J had the ball.

He had the ball now as he stood flexing his knees with nothing in front of him but open court. There was one dunk that no one had seen before. It existed in whispered playground myths. It existed in dreams. Even the all-stars watching from the side fell silent as they waited to see if the Doctor could dunk from the foul line, that stripe of paint 15 feet from the hoop.

He began sprinting downcourt toward the basket. "The arena was so quiet," said Scheer, "you could hear his every step as his shoes touched the floor."

Then his shoes were no longer touching the floor. There was nothing to hear. There was nothing to say. This was no dream.

Playgrounds from coast to coast buzzed with the news of Erving's foul-line dunk. Wherever ball was played at a breakneck pace with a premium on the astounding one-on-one move, Dr. J was king. Only the stodgy NBA, resentful of the exciting rival league that Erving had come to symbolize, refused to give him his full due as a player. Red Auerbach, longtime coach of the Boston Celtics, arrogantly dismissed the ABA star by saying, "Julius Erving is a nice kid, but he's not a great player."

NBA bosses like Auerbach had long felt that the playground style of basketball that Erving seemed to epitomize ran counter to the business of winning games. The Doctor was too flashy. The Doctor was a "hot dog." This line of thinking failed to account for one important fact: Julius Erving's teams always won.

ABA coaches, victimized on a nightly basis by Erving's brilliance, could not afford to be so ignorant. Al Bianchi, who coached Erving for two years before having to face the task of trying to stop him, pointed out that Erving's improvisations—what the NBA men called "hotdogging"—were always geared toward winning. "He doesn't do it to be a showman. He knows it will bring his team alive."

Erving referred to his style of play as "the play-ground game, refined." Erving refined the occasion-ally out-of-control playground game by parceling out his astounding moves throughout a contest like strategically timed explosions. "If we're down a few points and I'm fast-breaking," said the Doctor, "I'll sometimes decide that the time has come to get freaky."

Erving's "freaky" moves had the ability to deflate an opponent. Nelson George, in his book *Elevating the Game*, dubbed Erving a master of "intimidation through improvisation." Defenders began to believe the man was unstoppable. Even one of the greatest defensive forwards of all time, Bobby Jones, sounded like a defeatist when he talked of guarding Erving: "The thing about him is that you know he is going to get to the basket, you just never know how."

Coaches feared the moment when Erving would decide that the time had come. Bianchi said, "My whole defense against him is to stop him from going into his high-wire act. When he does that, his team gets excited and your players want to stop and applaud, too."

Hubie Brown went even farther than Bianchi in his defense against Erving. "We had a rule," said

Going all out on defense, Erving tries to prevent a layup by the Lakers' Jamaal Wilkes in 1980. When he joined the Philadelphia 76ers in 1976, Erving reined in his offensive genius in order to become a consistent all-around player and blend with the other marquee talents on the Sixers squad.

the Kentucky coach. "If Dr. J was coming down on the fast break, foul him. I didn't care if he was twenty feet from the basket. Just foul him before he took off. If you didn't foul him and Julius dunked, it was a $50 fine." Brown knew that a Dr. J dunk could turn any game into a one-man exhibition, with hometown fans abandoning their allegiances to cheer for Erving, defenders suddenly growing weak in the knees, and Erving's energized teammates gearing up as if ready to conquer the world. Even Brown was affected by the Doctor. In a voice that quavered unmistakeably with surrender, the veteran coach admitted, "I was in awe of what the guy could do."

Some people were still not convinced. Even after Erving joined the NBA in 1976 and continued his winning ways by leading the Philadelphia 76ers to the finals, Red Auerbach said, "In our league he's just another small forward." The cigar-chomping cur-mudgeon was joined in this hazy opinion by a mere handful. The legendary Dr. J, who had been known to most only by word of mouth, was beginning to take his rightful place at center stage.

The time had come. Ten years after his Rucker League debut, where he wowed the playground ex-perts, and four years after his Denver foul-line dunk, which sent the professional experts on hand into ecstasy, Erving was about to show everyone once and for all what it meant to get freaky.

TV cameras beaming the game to households all over the country followed the ball into Dr. J's enor-mous hands. It was Game 4 of the 1980 NBA finals, and Erving's Philadelphia 76ers, after squandering a large lead, were clinging to a precarious four-point edge over the Los Angeles Lakers late in the fourth quarter. Erving's defender, a human mountain named Mark Landsberger, rumbled over to cut off the lane to the hoop. Behind him, the Laker's superstar center, Kareem Abdul-Jabbar, edged away from his man, keying on Dr. J. The Doctor crouched and eyed the basket.

One lightning-fast step dusted Landsberger. "Then," said Erving, "I saw Kareem coming and waving his arms." Erving invited the agile giant into the Doctor's domain, up above the rim.

To lose Abdul-Jabbar, Erving pumped once at the right-hand side of the hoop and soared past the backboard, toward the crowd of photographers camped under the basket. The flashbulbs popped as Erving twisted, changing direction as smoothly as a bird, and skied across the baseline.

For the space of a heartbeat, Erving seemed to tread on the white flood of flashing light from the cameras. Abdul-Jabbar flailed at empty space. Behind the big man, on the left side of the hoop, Erving polished off the impossible reverse with a kiss, touching a scoop shot high and soft off the glass. The ball spun through the net, Erving alighted, and the game was won.

"There has never been a player like this guy," remarked Erving's coach, Billy Cunningham. Only the Doctor could win games like that. Only the Doctor could turn a tiny opening on the baseline into the door to a place where gravity surrenders. ❧

2

"GERONIMO!"

ON FEBRUARY 22, 1950, Callie Mae Erving gave birth to her second child, a son. Because it was Washington's Birthday, a nurse suggested that Mrs. Erving name the newborn after America's first president. Callie Mae replied, "Have your own baby if you want to name him George Washington. I'm naming mine Julius Winfield Erving, the Second."

When it came to raising the boy she called June (short for Junior), as well as his younger brother Marvin and older sister Alexis, Callie Mae Erving was in charge. The daughter of hardworking South Carolina sharecroppers, Mrs. Erving had seen enough of life to realize that if she failed to take charge, nobody else would. Her notion proved prophetic. Four years after June was born, the children's father moved out, and the task of guiding the three youngsters into the world fell solely on Callie Mae's shoulders.

"I made no plans for the children," she recalled. "I just prayed that things would turn out for them." The strength of Mrs. Erving's religious faith helped buoy her during difficult times. She was tireless, earning money as a housecleaner from morning until dusk, while acting as both mother and father to the children every other waking moment.

"I worked days, so I only had evenings to spend with them," she said. She made these rare hours count. If the difficult task of disciplining June, Alexis, or little Marvin arose, Callie Mae did not shirk it. She did the hard work. "I learned early," her eldest son later said, "that when I made a wrong decision I

Eleven-year-old Julius Erving holds his trophy after sparking his Salvation Army team to the championship in a Long Island youth league. A quiet youngster who kept his emotions bottled up, Julius learned to express his drive and creativity on the basketball court.

was punished. Conversely, doing the right thing always brought reward."

As June showed that he was absorbing her ideas of right and wrong, Callie Mae loosened her parental reins. "She let me do what I wanted," said Julius. "If I was wrong, I was willing to take the consequences." Watching his mother raise the family by herself taught Julius that self-reliance was necessary in a difficult world. Sometimes a person had to go it alone. He began stepping back and examining the world from a distance. "I consciously tried to be aware of what was happening around me," he said.

The family lived in a housing project on Linden Avenue in Hempstead, Long Island. Most of the people in the project were, like the Ervings, working hard just to get by. Times were not easy, but Callie Mae Erving was always upbeat. Her wish, as she described it, was to instill in her children "a desire to make each day better than the one before and to improve each task, however small."

As the children grew, it became apparent that she was succeeding. All three did well in school. Alexis and Marvin were the extroverts. Julius was the quiet one. Callie Mae knew that Julius was always thinking, biding his time, waiting for exactly the right moment to speak. But Alexis saw his reticence in a different light. "A lot of things happened where she thought I should react, but I didn't," Julius said of his older sister. "She told me one day that I was going to explode, holding things in so much." Alexis could not understand how anyone could go without talking. What she did not realize was that Julius was waiting for a way to express himself without using words.

One of Julius's early memories was of a game he and his friends played called Geronimo. It started one day at the swings. One boy, swinging as high as he could, suddenly vaulted from his seat, yelled "Geronimo!" and flew. When he thumped down on his feet in the dust, he whirled back to the others, a smile on his face, daring his friends to do what he had done. Everyone tried to top him, and soon enough a simple jump was not good enough. One boy twirled all the way around before landing. Another made his windbreaker into a parachute. Some tried for too much and crashed. Julius loved it. He realized that when he was flying, he could do things nobody else could do.

Like most games invented in the playground, this one was eventually ditched for some new pursuit. But Julius remembered the thrill of flying, and one day at the Campbell Park courts in Hempstead, he discovered another playground game. This one would not be so soon left behind.

The daring, creative, ferocious scores were what first drew Julius Erving to the game of basketball. "I loved to watch what guys would do in emergency situations," he said. The nine-year-old Julius studied the moments when a player, up in the air, surrounded by defenders, still found a way to get the ball in the hoop. Soon he was beating a path from his home to the courts at Campbell Park.

"I really didn't see June doing anything steadily until he took up playing ball," Callie Mae Erving said. The fervor with which Julius threw himself into the new pursuit indicated to Callie Mae that basketball could be more than just a game for her quiet son. Julius realized as much from the very start.

He took the court, and the rhythm of the ball on the blacktop thrummed up into his hands. The rim chattered when the shot was wrong. The chain net laughed when the shot was right. June played for hours on end, and the pent-up tension that his sister Alexis had once warned him about slowly unraveled into nothing. "When there was a fight at home or I was uptight," he said, "I would go down to the park and play, sometimes just by myself. And when I was through I would be feeling good again. I could come back and deal with the situation." Something began to come alive inside him when he went to the park to play. He could feel it like music humming through his bones. "Before I was physically able," Julius Erving said, "I felt these different things within me, certain moves, ways to dunk."

Alexis had said that her brother would some day explode, and in a way she was right. As the bony, gawky nine-year-old leaped and shoveled the ball at the basket, the explosive moves of the man called Dr. J rumbled inside him like the first tremors of an earthquake. "I realized all I had to do was be patient and they would come," he recalled. He began to experiment, finding out what worked and what did not. Sometimes it took a while for the moves he envisioned in his head to work on the court, but he said when they finally did, "I wasn't particularly surprised. They were a part of me for so long."

Julius had no one to guide him in his first experiments. Many other basketball stars tell of fathers or elder siblings pointing the way in their earliest days with the sport. Julius Erving started on his own. A child without his precocious self-confidence may have given up after one too many days when the shots would not fall. For Julius, the music flooding up inside him pushed him on when there was no one there to say, "Keep going."

"I set no dimensions for my game," he said. The pictures he had in his head of spectacular moves were allowed to flow untouched into the game as soon as his increasingly graceful limbs were ready. No coach was there to discourage what might be misinterpreted as a needlessly flashy move. By the time Julius finally came under the wing of his first coach, he had already discovered what was, for him, basketball's fundamental truth. "The pattern was set by then," he said. "I always went to the basket, that was my way." He

Erving's photograph in the Roosevelt High School yearbook conveys his serious and studious personality. Throughout his youth, Erving desired most of all to become a doctor and did not think of basketball as a possible career.

joined a Salvation Army team for 10- to 12-year-olds and found that winning came easy when he took the ball hard to the rack.

The team went 27-3 in his first year before rolling to a 31-1 record the following year. The young players traveled all over Long Island and even occasionally out of state. The world was beginning to open up to Julius. Rather than get swept away in the excitement of these first triumphs, he constantly sought out ways to reflect on what was happening to him. "Julius liked to find a church wherever we went," remembered his first coach, Don Ryan. Julius impressed Ryan as a youngster who would be much more than just a talented athlete. Memories of Julius winning a poetry recital contest took their place in the coach's mind alongside memories of Julius scoring a spectacular layup.

Although basketball touched a chord in him as nothing ever had, he never stopped thinking about the world beyond the playground. His consistent excellence in school caused his teacher to single him out in front of the class and ask him what he wanted to be when he grew up. Julius replied without pause, "I want to be a doctor."

When Julius was 11 years old, his father died. "He was struck by a car and killed," Julius remembered. "He didn't live with us, but still, now I didn't have a father, and even though he hadn't been around, now there was no possibility that he ever would be."

Callie Mae Erving and her children became closer than ever. When Julius was 14, his mother remarried, and the family moved to the nearby town of Roosevelt. Julius quickly found a place in the unfamiliar setting where he could turn "emergency situations" into triumphs.

At the courts in Roosevelt's Centennial Park, Julius threw himself into long hours of midair experimentation. He was not especially tall for his age, but already he could palm the ball, and he used this ability while practicing spinning, twirling layins and finger rolls. The game began to bow to his commands. "Dribbling the ball in junior high school, knowing I could pick the ball up in one hand off the dribble, or one hand off the backboard, changing my path while in the air—it all seemed pretty safe to me. I decided not to limit myself when I found I could do anything that I had ever seen any guy do."

A 14-year-old attacking the very limits of the game was bound to quickly attract attention. Earl

Ray Wilson, varsity basketball coach at Roosevelt High during the 1960s, first spotted Erving on the Hempstead playgrounds. "Watching him was like being in the presence of a great painter and seeing him create something new for you each day," he recalled.

Mosley, the coach of Roosevelt High School's freshman team, was one of the first to notice the new kid. What struck him immediately was that Julius "used to play with the junk shot. Twisting things, lobs and all kinds of spinning maneuvers."

The junk shot, hated by Mosley and most coaches as a chaotic form of total surrender, was being transformed into art by a teenager. Julius saw his junk-shot experiments as necessary. "I was always small," he said. "Yet I always had big hands and could jump, so I learned to be trickier than the big guys."

Earl Mosley became a believer. He said, "It wasn't long before Jewel—that's what we called him then—owned that park. Everyone wanted to play against him, especially the older and bigger kids." Julius's long hours of practice were put to the test as the playground challenges began in earnest. Ray Wilson, Roosevelt's varsity coach, watched intently, knowing that there was more at stake than just a game. "The whole playground thing is a means of expression," Wilson explained. "For black kids it's an important way of getting your contemporaries' approval. Life's all a struggle for pride. Second best is nothing. You've got to establish yourself as number one."

The score, as Julius already knew, was often incidental. "There's a whole psychology in the play-ground game," Julius said, "that makes you want to beat a guy in a way that makes him pay twice. You want to outscore him and you also want to freak him out with a big move or a big block. That way even if the score is tied, you and he both know you're really ahead."

The games raged at Centennial Park. Often the struggle for pride exploded. "Many of the games in that park ended in fights or arguments," recalled Mosley. "Most of the kids wanted to show they were the best with their fists." The best player rose above the fights. "Jewel never asserted himself by being brash or lewd, I never remember seeing him in a fight or an argument. He always asserted himself by creat-ing a move. He knew how good he was, but he never bragged about it. He got strength and love at home that a lot of others didn't get. His family was not financially well-off, but his mother's a strong woman. Culturally, Julius's family is rich."

Julius was wise enough not to jeopardize his blossoming art in any way. Mosley, who was the school principal in addition to being the freshman coach, recalled, "Julius was never a street hanger. He would never hang out drinking wine like so many other kids did. If you wanted Julius, you always knew where to find him—in the park or at school."

Julius continued to excel in school, still holding to his dream of becoming a doctor. Amazingly, the thought had yet to occur to him that he had a chance to play professional basketball. "To tell the truth," he said of his early exploits on the playgrounds, "I thought everybody could do those things." Those who watched from the side knew better. "Watching him," according to Ray Wilson, "was like being in the presence of a great painter and seeing him create something new for you each day."

Word began to spread of the new teenage king of Centennial Park. Julius began to travel to other playgrounds. Other players began to travel to him. Soon he was locking horns not only with the best of Roosevelt but the best of the entire New York metropolitan area.

The most famous high school player of that era was a graceful 7-footer from Harlem named Lew Alcindor. Just prior to the ferocious college recruiting war that would make Alcindor a household name from coast to coast, the big center spent the summer of 1965 on the playground. He played everywhere. He took on everyone. One day he met his match.

"Riis Park, up the Rockaway Peninsula," recalled Alcindor, now known as Kareem Abdul-Jabbar. "This skinny, bony kid. He didn't handle the ball much. Just rebounded. We measured hands once. His were bigger. He played up front, one-handed everything and stuffed over everybody." Abdul-Jabbar paused, holding in his mind the image of the Roosevelt teenager flying through the air, up where nobody else could go. "One summer, all of a sudden, there was Julius Erving." ❧

3

BECOMING FEARLESS

———— ◖◗ ————

 $\mathbf{I}$T WAS THE late fall of 1966, just days before the Roosevelt High School varsity took the floor for their first game. Ray Wilson had seen enough of his team's intense preseason scrimmages to realize that he had a problem most coaches would love to have. He had too many good players. Someone with talent enough to be a starter in any other year was going to have to go to the bench.

There were five seniors on the team who had played together since junior high school, and they were looking forward to their final year, when they would take the court together as the starting five. Their dream would have been realized without a hitch if not for the presence of a 6-foot-3-inch 11th grader who could practically jump out of the gym.

"He had to know he was the best player I had," said Wilson of the junior, Julius Erving. The easy choice would have been to start the most talented five. The coach understood, however, that winning takes more than pure talent. A disgruntled player on the bench often ruptures team unity. Wilson, a former college basketball star, had seen teams brought down by it. He had seen cliques and bad blood between teammates lead to an every-man-for-himself attitude on the court.

Luckily, Wilson had a player in Julius Erving who understood as well as any coach what makes a succesful team. "I knew he could come off the bench and handle it, while some of the others could not," Wilson said. "Julius is of the nature that he will do whatever is necessary to win at the expense of individual glory."

During his years on the Roosevelt High varsity, Erving won admiration not only for his scoring but also for his leadership and his unselfish attitude. Though he was clearly Roosevelt's number one star, he always placed the good of the team ahead of his personal goals.

Wilson knew how rare Erving's ability to handle the situation was. "Most kids in his place would've quit because they would've felt that their friends thought them fools to do all that practicing only to play second string. Julius never had those hang-ups. He never had to dominate a situation, so he was never a threat to anybody. He always had that inner security."

Erving knew it was best for the team that he take his benching without complaint. He did not need the essentially meaningless honor of being on the starting five. He was confident enough to wait for the coach to call his name.

The call usually came sometime in the second quarter of every game that year. A writer at a Roosevelt game recalled that shortly after Erving shed his warm-up suit, "the whole rhythm of the game changed." The plodding style that Roosevelt's five seniors employed shifted almost imperceptibly to accomodate the daring end-to-end forays of "a young boy with the body control of an accomplished ballet dancer."

As the season went on the seniors looked to Erving more and more. He took over the team scoring lead, finishing with an 18-points-per-game average, while also leading the team in rebounds. By year's end, with Roosevelt rumbling into the playoffs, the seniors, who could have easily learned to resent the junior had he complained about his benching, had unofficially bestowed upon Erving the title of team leader.

The next year, it was Julius Erving's team from the start. He did not, however, challenge Wilson's authority, as some star players are wont to do. In fact, he went out of his way to uphold that authority. Once, Erving missed a bus to a practice scrimmage because he and his friends had stopped to help a woman dig her car out of the snow. Rather than talk back to the coach and explain his lateness, Erving elected to accept Wilson's punishment of a one-game suspension quietly. The team, following Erving's model of noble reticence, gelled quickly into a formidable unit under coach Wilson.

Though Erving would lead the team in scoring and rebounding, he was not a one-man gang. Two accomplished players from New York City, Tommy Taylor, a 6-foot-3-inch guard, and George Green, a 6-foot-6-inch forward, had transferred to Roosevelt over the summer for their senior year. Green, a mobile, sharpshooting big man, actually garnered more attention than Erving from college scouts who perused the high school games. Again sensing what was best for the team, Erving concentrated on crashing the boards while Taylor and Green shot from the outside. The threesome, who had learned how to play together during the summer in playground games all over the metropolitan area, turned the Roosevelt High varsity into a juggernaut.

Julius's family members were among the biggest rooters as the team rolled to a 16-1 regular season mark. Erving's biggest fan at that time, in fact, was his brother Marvin. Marvin, who had battled various illnesses all his life, saw in Julius the athlete he could never be. Julius in turn saw qualities in Marvin that he himself lacked. "Marvin was an extrovert," said Julius. "I admired him for that." Exhibiting the self-confidence that Callie Mae Erving instilled in all her children, Marvin saw a future of brilliant triumph for himself and his brother, envisioning Julius as a professional athlete and himself as a U.S. senator.

Julius, for his part, did not get carried away with grandiose thoughts about the future. At the time, he was unaware of how far he could go. "I never considered pro ball a reality," he said. The limited scope of this view, not to be confused with underconfidence, carried over to Julius's thoughts about his

As a member of the University of Massachusetts squad, Erving drives the lane against Boston College. When he enrolled at UMass in 1969, Erving was concerned more with getting a solid education than with becoming a big-time basketball player.

team. "My perspective was entirely local. Our team at Roosevelt High School could have been the best in the country. In the country! But we had no idea. Our ultimate aim was to win the Nassau County championship."

In the first round of the playoffs, Roosevelt stomped in the direction of that goal, routing the overmatched competition 82–48. Erving led the way with 28 points and 11 rebounds. In the next round, a team from Elmont Memorial turned the game into a slow-paced, foul-ridden wrestling match. Roosevelt could not rise above it, mustering only 49 points to Elmont's 62 by the time the final buzzer sounded.

The stunning loss did not break Erving's spirit. Feeding off of Marvin's big dreams, Julius looked toward the future. As his last year in high school wound to a close, he came to his mother with a promise. "This is just the beginning," he told Callie Mae. "I mean to go far."

He soon attracted wider attention. A burly NBA center named Wayne Embry spent the summer of 1968 at a remote basketball camp in Upstate New York. One afternoon, as he was shooting baskets by himself in the camp's deserted gym, he was approached by one of the camp's coaches. The coach had someone he thought Embry should play. "The kid came onto the court," remembers Embry, "and he was about 6-foot-5 and pretty skinny, but he had big hands. He introduced himself as Julius Erving, which meant nothing to me."

Embry was no stranger to tough competition. After a long stint as a starter for the Oscar Robertson–led Cincinatti Royals, he had become Bill Russell's backup on the world champion Boston Celtics. When he was not spelling Russell in games, he was tangling with the Hall of Famer on a daily basis in practice. Having held his own with the best, he naturally assumed that a high school kid would pose no challenge.

Embry handicapped himself with a special set of rules for the one-on-one match. "I had to shoot outside and the kid could do whatever he wanted, which is exactly what he did to me—whatever he wanted. He was absolutely phenomenal. I kept looking at him and couldn't believe he was a high school kid. His hands weren't just big, they were enormous."

Using the special rules, Julius repeatedly trounced the NBA veteran. Finally Embry's pride began to hurt. "I'm going inside," announced the man who held a 4-inch, 70-pound size advantage. "I was going to muscle this skinny kid," Embry recalled, "but I couldn't catch him. He drove around me, he dunked over me. I was an NBA center and I had lost to a high school kid." Aware that misery loves company, Embry sought out another NBA player at the camp, a high-scoring forward named Johnny Green. "I got Julius and turned him loose on Jumping Johnny Green, as he was known back then. But Johnny found out who could really jump and Julius kicked his butt, too."

Embry and Green notwithstanding, Julius Erving remained unknown to most of the basketball world. Local colleges like Manhattan, Hofstra, and St. John's showed interest. Colleges like Cleveland State and Iowa with traditionally weak basketball programs also attempted to recruit Erving. For the most part, however, he was spared the siege of recruiters that often surrounds today's high school stars.

Erving also remained something of a secret to himself. His promise to his mother that he would go far did not, in his mind, refer to basketball. The levelheaded teen instead adhered to a plan that would bring him success beyond the game. "I had a list of priorities then," he said. "First was school; second, social life; third, basketball."

These priorities helped guide Erving in his choice of a college. Also weighing on his mind was a desire to stay relatively close to Roosevelt and his family. Alexis was planning to get married and move away, and Marvin, who was seldom in good health, seemed to be getting sick even more often than usual. Ultimately, Erving leaned on Coach Wilson when the final choice was to be made. "I went to the University of Massachusetts," Erving says, "mainly because Ray Wilson was a friend of Jack Leaman, the UMass coach."

The small town of Amherst, Massachusetts, where the university was located, was a nice fit for the quiet, meditative new freshman. He was able to

Erving poses with UMass head coach Jack Leaman in 1970. Leaman's friendship with Roosevelt High coach Ray Wilson was a major factor in Erving's decision to attend UMass.

concentrate immediately on both his studies and his "third priority," basketball.

Word quickly spread that there was a new kid on campus who could play some ball. Even before the season started, fans braved the 90-degree heat of the Boyden Building gym to watch Erving work out. During these workouts, Erving concentrated mostly on improving the weakest part of his game, his outside shot. He did not yet understand why there were people scattered among the bleachers. But he did note that they seemed to perk up when he broke from his perimeter shooting drills to throw down a few thunderclap jams.

In 1968, freshmen were not allowed to play varsity, as they are now. The rule was meant to give freshman a year away from the limelight of major college ball to get acclimated to the college environment. At UMass, however, the limelight found Julius Erving anyway. Though the varsity team was on their way to a fine 18-6 mark for the season, it was the freshman team that truly captured the fans' imaginations. Lines for tickets to see the undefeated freshman team play started forming three hours before game time. The star of the team began to realize that the throng coming to see him every night might be onto something.

"That's when I started hearing all these people talking about how different I was supposed to be," Erving said. "It was a shock, but when a hundred people tell you you're different, then a thousand people tell you you're different, you just say to yourself, 'Okay, I'm different.' "

It was Marvin's idea to go to the game. He badgered Callie Mae in the days leading up to his brother's birthday until she finally agreed to take him to Amherst for a surprise visit. When Callie Mae and Marvin arrived on February 22, they squeezed in with the rest of the crowd to watch the invincible freshmen play.

"At halftime," Callie Mae recalled, "the spectators and the team sang 'Happy Birthday' for Julius and I was so very proud and happy." The world was falling in love with her eldest boy. After they left Amherst to return home, Callie Mae soon realized that she could not be so secure about the baby of the family.

"On the way back to New York we were caught in the worst snowstorm I can remember," she said, "and the very next day Marvin began complaining that his arms and knees hurt." When Julius came home for spring break a few weeks later, Marvin was in the hospital with an ailment initially diagnosed as arthritis. Later, the doctors determined that Marvin had lupus erythematosus, a fatal disease affecting the bloodstream.

"He had always been sickly, so I never thought it was serious," Julius said later. "But somehow my mother must have known because the night before I went back to school she cried and cried." The day he returned to college he got a call from home. Marvin was barely holding on. The possibility that Julius refused to admit was coming true. His brother was dying. Nothing could get him home fast enough.

The last of the snow that had papered the frozen ground for months melted in the rising spring sun. Brown grass began to reach toward the light. The world roused from its frozen slumber. "At 19 I lost my brother," Julius Erving said, "the only brother that I had." It was the spring of 1969, and Erving found himself where he had been the day before, and the day before that. He found himself among the graves: "I cried all day on the day of the funeral. I went to the cemetery the first few days after he was buried and I cried each day. I told myself I wasn't going to cry anymore, ever. I was really brought to my knees and made to feel helpless and powerless. It was like I no longer had control. I could be gone tomorrow."

Julius spent the summer back home with his mother. He got a job in Hempstead, looking after the courts at his old stamping ground, Campbell Park. After the games had all broken up, Julius took the court as he had when he was nine years old.

He knew the pain of Marvin's death would never go away, and he knew his own life could end in an instant. He played ball among the long shadows. The chain net ticked off the hours of the night. The ball wired a pulse from the black asphalt to his fingertips. He could feel his heart pumping a reply in his chest. He knew what he had to do.

"I felt helpless," Erving says, recalling the midnight hours following Marvin's death, "but I also became fearless." Julius Erving realized that there was no reason, in this brief life, to ever hold anything back. "I felt, 'Well, if I'm going to do something I'm going to let it all hang out.' " ❧

4

"THE CHAINS WERE OFF"

THE UMASS MINUTEMEN reeled off 13 straight victories early on in the 1969–70 season. Julius Erving played like a man among boys. In a game against Boston University he scored 29 points and corralled 20 rebounds in the first half. Told at halftime that he had a great shot at breaking the school's single-game record for both points and rebounds, Erving went out in the second half and dished out 15 assists. "If I broke the record tonight," he explained to his coach, "what would I have to shoot for in the next two years?"

The team finished with an 18-7 record, good enough for a berth in the National Invitational Tournament (NIT) at Madison Square Garden in New York. The NIT, once the toughest tournament in the country, has since taken a backseat to the National Collegiate Athletic Association (NCAA) tournament. In 1970, however, the NIT boasted as its top-seeded team a genuine national power. Al McGuire's Marquette team had rejected the NCAA tournament for what it saw as a slight. They expected their easy ride to the NIT finals to start with a drubbing of the team from UMass.

Marquette ultimately squeezed out a five-point win, but they had to survive a shocking start during which the Minutemen scored the first 12 points. At that point, Marquette's excitable coach ripped his jacket off, flung his clipboard to the floor, and snapped his hands into a T. As his stunned starting five filed to the bench for the time-out, Al McGuire started shouting. "Who the hell is that kid out there!"

As a UMass junior, Erving led the varsity to its best record in school history as he averaged 26.9 points and 19.5 rebounds per game.

45

Erving (32) first caught the eye of pro scouts during the 1970 National Invitational Tournament (NIT) at Madison Square Garden, when UMass threw a scare into heavily favored Marquette, losing to the eventual tournament champions by only five points.

he yelled, jabbing a finger at the player who had led the underdog team's opening charge.

"That's Julius, coach," said one of McGuire's assistants.

"Julius who? What d'ya mean Julius? How come I didn't know about this guy?"

College basketball's best-kept secret spent the following summer traveling from playground to playground in a rusty, dented, gas-guzzling Chevy. One day at Richie O'Conner Park in Queens, Erving matched up in a full-court game with Dave Stallworth, a reserve forward with the New York Knicks.

On the first play, Erving burst past Stallworth on the left and dunked. The next time down he faked left and drove right, again beating Stallworth to the hole for a slam. Erving's friend Dave Brownbill recalls, "Stallworth was getting pissed off. He started to lean on Julius and push him around. But whenever he leaned on him, Julius rolled the other way and easily went to the hoop. The two of them played to a standoff, the big star from the world champion Knicks and the college kid from some unknown school."

As Brownbill and Erving rode out of Queens in the rattling Chevy, a realization began to emerge. "That day," Brownbill says, "Julius found out how good he was."

This lesson was reinforced as the summer stretched on. He was invited in as a last-minute replacement at the Olympic development camp in Colorado. "There I was with guys like Paul Westphal, an all-American from USC, Tom McMillan from Maryland, Joby Wright from Indiana." The sophomore from the small-time New England team was in awe of the well-known college stars. "I never considered that I could play on the level of guys from UCLA or Purdue," he said. "Well, I led the team in scoring and rebounding and I began to think, Hmmm. *Maybe.*"

Back home on Long Island, Erving kept traveling around, playing ball, leaving behind a black cloud of exhaust and a buzz in the crowd wherever he went. "All the talk," remembered Dave Brownbill, "was about this kid Julius, and how he was making all the pros look bad in the parks." As the summer ended, Erving's beat-up Chevy was stolen. "No one would have wanted the car," said Brownbill. "They must have stolen it for all the trophies in the back."

In his junior year, Erving led UMass to a record of 23-3, the best in the school's history. By now he was not so much driving to the basket as attacking it. His above-the-rim style was truly fearless, though some stunned watchers were moved to view it as downright fearsome.

"I'm afraid to write what I saw," said one reporter who had just seen a UMass game. "He got the ball in the corner, took one step and was at the basket. *On the other side!*" "You better not write that," the reporter's colleague replied.

Erving, showing the Yankee Conference crowds something new every night, averaged 26.9 points and 19.5 rebounds a game. "He was a great passer, too," said his coach, Jack Leaman. "He could hit a man at three-quarter court during the fast break and he was a standout on defense. He could have scored a lot more," asserted the coach, whose team played a controlled brand of basketball. UMass eschewed the fast break in most situations to instead walk the ball up and slowly pound it inside. "We made Julius play team offense and team defense. We set it up so that he could handle a lot of situations he would face in the pros, situations that many college hotshots had trouble handling."

While Leaman's game plan helped Erving in the long run, it also helped keep him a secret. Had UMass employed a fast-breaking, gun-it-up style, Erving would probably have led the nation in scoring. As it was, he remained unknown to most. A chance to excel in the national spotlight finally presented itself when UMass squared off against a powerful University of North Carolina team in the first round of the NIT. Now the scouts were watching. Erving, however, had a rare off-game, getting in foul trouble early and never becoming a factor in a season-ending loss.

The dubious performance was enough to make most of the scouts forget about the kid from UMass. But a couple of watchers took a closer look. "He didn't play that much," recalls Al Bianchi, then

coach of the ABA franchise in Virginia, "but we could tell that he was pretty damn good."

At this time the ABA, desperate for star players, was raiding the undergraduate college ranks. Jack Leaman did not feel that he had anything to worry about. "The pros never looked at New England ballplayers, especially when they were only juniors."

Leaman's level of shock when the Virginia Squires approached Erving with an offer was rivaled only by the surprise that Erving felt himself. For Erving, it was the final blow to his sober-minded concept of the future that had defined basketball as nothing more than a game. "The offer made me start thinking about how many hours I had spent playing

Erving watches helplessly as a North Carolina player goes in for an easy layup during the 1971 NIT. Despite a 23-3 season, UMass was no match for the powerful Tar Heels, who won the game by 41 points and went on to capture the NIT crown.

ball. I was amazed. I had to admit to myself that basketball meant more than I thought it did."

The game that had already given him countless hours of pure joy now held the key to his future. "It was a chance to change my financial situation for life. I felt I had accomplished all I could in college ball and I was ready to turn pro." The young man had turned it over in his mind many times. He had considered all the options. Now there remained only one thing to do before he set out for new horizons by signing his name on the dotted line of a pro contract. "Well, first I called home to make sure it was okay," he admitted.

Erving's new stamping ground, the ABA, was aptly defined by broadcaster Bob Costas, who when thinking back to his days as a 20-year-old play-by-play man for the St. Louis Spirits, dubbed the league "basketball's Wild West." A certain lawless feeling, a premonition that anything could, and probably would, happen, was as constant in the ABA as tumbleweed in a western ghost town.

One of the early architects of the renegade league was an Indiana attorney named Dick Tinkham, who later admitted, "We went by the seat of our pants and made it up as we went along. If a rule didn't fit with something we wanted to do, we just changed it or ignored it. If someone had an idea, no matter how lame-brained, usually someone tried it."

Team owners changed the traditional brown color of the ball to splashy, patriotic red, white, and blue. They instituted the three-point shot. They had massive merchandise giveaways to get people into the arenas. Halftime might feature a cow-milking contest, and country music jamborees were common after games. A team in Dallas had as their mascot a voluptuous 6-foot-7-inch woman known as Miss Tall Texan. The Miami franchise hired five tanned, long-legged women to serve as bikini-clad ball girls.

Games were delayed when team uniforms got lost at the cleaners. Games were canceled when the home team realized that their arena had already been booked by a traveling circus.

In the beginning, teams were so desparate for players that they held open tryouts, inviting thousands of hopefuls into the broken-down barnlike arenas where they planned to play their games. One team signed a player right out of prison, only to let him go after he revealed a penchant for waking up his road roommate by pointing a pistol at his head. Another team, ravaged by injuries, pulled a man out of their public relations department and sent him into a game.

Flaky characters were the norm, rather than the exception, on team rosters. The best team in the league, the Indiana Pacers, had a front line that featured, in turn: A center who burst through the locker-room door every day dressed like a cowboy, complete with sharpened spurs and gleaming, fully loaded six-shooter pistols; a roisterous power forward who brought his pet lion along with him when he went out for his nightly dose of revelry; and a small forward who was convinced he could mesmerize his defender by dribbling the multicolored ball a special way.

The ABA would try anything once, and more often than not, their daringness paid off. The three-point shot, the tallying of statistics like blocked shots and steals, and the slam-dunk contest were all born in basketball's Wild West. "But the real flair," Bob Costas is quick to point out, "was on the court." The playground game, frowned upon in the NBA, was allowed to thrive in the arenas of the ABA. "The ABA players and coaches forced a faster pace of the game," said former Carolina Cougar Billy Cunningham, "they pushed the ball up the court, they created a more exciting brand of basketball, the kind of basketball you see in most of the NBA today."

"The NBA was a symphony, it was scripted," added player agent Ron Grinker. "The ABA was jazz." On every level, from the owners to the players, the ABA fed on the same spontaneity and passion that fuels the wailing jazz solo. Teams were always on the lookout for those who could play the soaring music. Dr. J and the ABA were a perfect fit from the start.

Different people noticed different things about the rookie from UMass. Al Bianchi, getting his first look in person at Julius Erving, and more specifically at Erving's hands, grabbed the arm of the man beside him and exclaimed, "My God, did you see those meat hooks!"

"The first thing I noticed," offered Virginia Squires forward George Irvine, "was his Afro. It was the biggest Afro I had ever seen." In a league that featured players such as Darnell Hillman, whose billowing hairdo earned him the nickname Eclipse, this was no minor achievement.

But such cosmetic details fade in the memory of the Squires general manager, Johnny Kerr. His first memory of Julius Erving started with a sharp, ricochet sound. It happened at the Squires' summer tryout camp. "A shot banged against the back of the rim and went straight up," he said. "It was one of those rebounds where it seems that all five players were jumping for it. Out of the middle of the pack came Julius . . . up . . . up . . . up. He cupped the rebound with one hand and then slammed it through the rim, all in one motion. The gym went silent. All the players just stopped for a few seconds. This was a tryout camp and I had just watched one of the best plays I had ever seen in my life."

Julius Erving entered the ABA dunking. At that time, colleges and high schools had outlawed the dunk. "I hadn't been allowed to dunk in competition for four years," Erving recalled. When he got to the pros, "the chains were off. At first I couldn't get enough of it."

His teammates could not get enough of it either. "I never had a bench that was more attentive than when Doc played for me," says Bianchi, "because the guys wanted to watch the game to see what he would do next." The unfettered rookie tore through the league on a mad, dunking rampage.

"I was 21, out of the college environment and out on my own for the first time," the Doctor reflected. "And I loved every minute of it. Basketball was truly a game, there were few hassles, and on the court we were freewheeling." Erving jetted from city to city, unleashing his blistering slams. And every time he made the rims rattle and the fans howl, Squires back-up center Willie Sojourner would taunt the torched opposition from the bench: "There's the Doctor digging into his bag again!"

The spectacular rookie operated at a less raucous pitch away from the court. "He was friendly but very quiet," said George Irvine of Erving's early days in the pros. "For a while he just sat and watched." Erving's thoughtful, contemplative demeanor, as well as his spectacular on-court skills, moved the ABA veteran Doug Moe to proclaim, "Julius was the most mature rookie I've ever seen."

Erving's maturity was put the test by the mind-bogglingly selfish play of teammate Charlie Scott. The skyrocketing popularity of the rookie gnawed at Scott, who was used to being the star of the show. "To balance Julie's dominance," says Al Bianchi, "Charlie wanted to win the league scoring title. I knew it. He knew it. Julie knew it. Julie was mature enough to accept it and to fit his game to the fact."

As Scott expanded the already voluminous bounds of the basketball term "gunner" by hoisting an average of 30 shots per game, Erving dutifully crashed the boards. He averaged 15.7 rebounds a game in 1971–72, good for third in the league behind two hulking centers, Mel Daniels and Artis Gilmore. Despite Scott's ball hogging, he also managed to score 27.3 points per game, an outstanding mark for anyone, stunning for a rookie. When Scott bolted for the NBA just before the playoffs, Erving became a one-man wrecking crew, playing 46 minutes a game and leading all postseason players in rebounds, scoring, and assists.

By the end of his first campaign, Erving began to examine the less artful side of pro basketball. The pragmatic young man realized quite correctly that he was playing as well as anyone in the league, and yet he was not getting paid like the all-star that he was. The Atlanta Hawks of the NBA joined in the ongoing interleague war by making Erving a better offer. Erving listened. In the uproar that followed his signing with the NBA team, he offered a cogent explanatory statement that belied his age: "The life of a pro athlete is a short one."

The transformation of a naive college kid just happy to be playing basketball to a man in charge of his financial future was not without its painful side effects. A harsh legal battle ensued between Erving, the Squires, the Hawks, and the Milwaukee Bucks, who held Erving's NBA draft rights. Erving did not flinch in the face of these difficulties. "I invited myself into this situation," he said, "and I'm willing to pay the consequences."

A federal court ruled that while the case went to arbitration, Erving would have to play for Virginia for another year. "In effect," pointed out Squires owner Earl Foreman, "he lost." Many other players would have let bitterness over the setback seep into their on-court attitude, but that was not Erving's style. "Julius had a great second year for us while his case went to arbitration. The off-the-court

In the uniform of the Virginia Squires, Erving shoots over New York's John Baum during the 1972 ABA playoffs. After averaging 27.3 points a game during the regular season, Erving led all ABA scorers during the playoffs with a phenomenal 33.3 average.

stuff never bothered him," said Foreman, adding, "He was a classy guy in every way."

"Julius was even better in his second year with us," agreed Al Bianchi. "Now he was starting to get an idea how to play." Bianchi's facetious understatement bears a grain of truth about Erving's further maturation. Erving realized that by reining in his tornado of whirling slams and flying blocks he could have an even greater effect on a game. The rookie mistakes—fumbled passes, ill-advised forays, cheap fouls—disappeared. The tornado began to heed his call.

"Last year he used to blow my mind with a new move about three times a game," Erving's frontcourt mate Neil Johnson said. "Now it's only once a game that he'll do something that will leave the guys on the bench looking at each other and just sort of shaking their heads." Erving, who admitted that "as I get older my game gets more conservative," was in the process of refining the playground game. He acknowledged that the playground emphasis on one-on-one humiliation "used to dominate my thinking in informal game situations, but I feel I've been very fortunate that it has never been part of my concept of how a formal, five-man game should be played. I honestly feel there are guys in the pros who have never stopped thinking that way and it restricts their usefulness. They may end up as high scorers, but they haven't helped their teams."

As Erving translated his individually spectacular playground skills into a devastating team-oriented plan of attack, he began to expand the limits of the pro game. Before the Doctor arrived, pros were divided into two categories: big men who rebounded, blocked shots, and shot from close to the basket; and small men who handled the ball and shot from the outside.

"What I've tried to do," said Erving a few years later, "is merge those two types of games . . . and combine them in the same player. This has more or less changed the definition of what's called the small forward position, and it creates a lot more flexibility for the individual player, and, of course, creates a lot more opportunities for the whole team." The pro game of the 1990s, dominated by mobile, do-it-all wingmen like Michael Jordan, Charles Barkley, Clyde Drexler, Larry Bird, Dominique Wilkins, Larry Johnson, Chris Mullin, and Scottie Pippen, was pioneered 20 years earlier by the Doctor.

Erving did not really set out to be a trailblazer for the star players of the future. His deepest motives for playing the game were revealed as he left the Squires for the New York Nets just prior to the 1973–74 season. The complicated arbitration case was resolved when the Nets purchased Erving's contract from Virginia and paid the Hawks $1 million in compensation. Replying to a reporter's question about media pressure, Erving said, "I put the most pressure on myself because of my ambition to be the best basketball player ever. What happens around me can't put any more pressure on me than that." ❦

5

KING OF NEW YORK

ULIUS ERVING'S FIRST day as a Net went so well that it almost doomed his team to a season in the cellar. "The first practice, we saw how good he could be," said assistant coach Rod Thorn. "Julius just dominated the practice defensively. He made steal after steal, taking away guys' dribbles, picking off passes, and it seemed that with those long arms and huge hands he came up with every loose ball. I had never seen a guy with such athleticism."

Erving's performance prompted coach Kevin Loughery to dream up an attacking full-court press for his team to use all game long. "My original concept seemed perfectly suited to the Doctor. He plays so hard, so fast." The Nets won four of their first five games, but then the fatigue due to pressing from the opening tap to the final buzzer started to show in the faces of all the Nets, Dr. J included.

The Nets began to lose in the worst imaginable ways, handing out fourth-quarter leads like Halloween candy. The losing streak hit 10 in Utah, as Erving managed a mere 9 points in 22 ineffectual minutes. The Nets were in last place as they flew into San Diego. The sun-drenched purgatory of southern California was the place where the team would decide whether their season would live or die.

The Nets' desperation-inspired closed-door meeting before their game with the San Diego Conquistadors was the turning point of the season. "The coaches challenged the players," Erving said, "and then turned around and pointed a finger at themselves."

Dressed in the height of 1970s fashion, Erving palms the trademark red-white-and-blue ABA ball during a 1973 press conference. At the conference, the New York Nets announced that they had acquired the star forward's contract.

Loughery was not too proud to shoulder the blame. Speaking of his full-court press, he said, "No one can play that way for 84 games." He realized that he would have to find a better way to utilize Erving's talents because, as he said, "I was in the process of destroying the best player on my team, maybe the game."

The Nets came out of the meeting ready to make several strategic changes. The experience also served as a collective gut check. One of the many young, inexperienced players on the team, a guard named Brian Taylor, characterized the discussion as "cold and hard." An uncompromising sense of honesty, humility, and self-sacrifice, difficult to swallow at first, began to take hold in the Nets' locker room.

Loughery reined in the full-court press, deciding to spring it on the opposition only when necessary. He devised a sagging half-court man-to-man defense that would allow Erving to roam from his man to pick off errant passes. "As we went along," Loughery said, "I learned how to use the Doctor. We set up plays to have Doc get the ball on the move."

Erving averaged over 30 points a game as the Nets took off, winning 19 of the 22 games following their San Diego meeting. While Erving took control on the court, he also took control, in a much less spectacular fashion, of the nebulous aspect of a team's success known as chemistry.

"The reputation of the Nets last year," Erving said at the time, "was that if you got up on them early they'd start squabbling among themselves. They were losers. From the minute I knew I was coming I was preparing to stop that from happening again."

Erving led by example, working hard in practice and performing with inspiring grace and passion in games. He also subtly fostered a more positive feeling among his teammates. "There has to be criticism among players on a team," he said, "but I guess what

Erving ignites a fast break in a 1974 game against his former Virginia teammates. The up-tempo, run-and-gun style of the ABA was ideally suited to the Doctor's explosive athleticism.

I've tried to do is make it constructive and cut down on the meaningless griping at each other. I don't think you should cuss at a guy for missing a pass. You should boost him up by saying something like, 'It's all right. We'll get it next time.' "

Erving did not hold himself above any of the other players, which Rod Thorn saw as "a big factor in our success. Kevin found he could criticize Julius and Julius would not turn on him like most stars. In fact, I know that sometimes Kevin would scream at Doc just to let the other guys know that Doc was no different than they were."

Erving also went out of his way to bolster the confidence of young players on the team. When Larry "Mr. K" Kenon, who played opposite Erving in the frontcourt, hit a rough stretch in his rookie season,

Erving took Thorn aside and told him, "Don't worry about Kenon. I'll take care of him." In the game that followed, Erving repeatedly drew the defense with drives and then dished the ball to his wide-open rookie teammate. Thorn remembered, "Kenon ended up with a 30-point night and was all smiles. After the game, Julius told reporters about how great Kenon had played and how Kenon was very important to the team."

Kenon, a lithe 6-foot-10-inch leaper, developed into the perfect foil for Erving. If teams keyed too heavily on Dr. J, Mr. K would go to work. He could stick short jumpers all day long, and he could also blast to the hoop for the slam. For opposing teams, the most fearsome sight in the league was both men out on the break, Dr. J gliding down on the right lane, Mr. K matching him step for step on the left. Stopping this kind of Nets break was like trying to stop an electrical storm.

Rounding out the frontcourt for the Nets was the extremely round Billy Paultz, known to his fans as the Whopper. The sagging, slope-shouldered Paultz, who resembled a 6-foot-11-inch pile of melted candle wax, was a far cry from anyone's ideal of athletic heartiness. But he managed to give the Nets a credible low-post scoring threat and also, of course, clogged up the middle quite well on defense. Woe to the opposing player who drove the lane, hoping for a layup, only to be whopped by the Whopper.

In the backcourt, the Nets had a little fire and a little ice. John Williamson provided the fire. He was described by Nets announcer Steve Albert as "more of a warrior than a player, a guy who went out there and physically punished you." On top of using his football player's build to his advantage, Super John, a wildly streaky shooter, could single-handedly win games if he got hot. Williamson's backcourt mate, the consistent, levelheaded Brian Taylor, ran the show from the point. When the game was on the line, the poised second-year man always seemed to have ice water running in his veins.

After the all-star break, the Nets made a deal that shored up their team, sending John Roche to Kentucky for ball-hawking guard Mike Gale and 6-foot-5-inch forward Wendell Ladner. Ladner played basketball like a large boulder rolling down a hill. His defining moment had occurred in the playoffs the year before when he dove for a loose ball and crashed into a watercooler. The shattered glass left a gash in his head that required 38 stitches, but Ladner was back on the bench in the second half, begging the coach to let him play. Ladner's 220 pounds of pure hustle were just what the Nets needed coming off their bench. He also quickly adopted a more nefarious role with something just short of glee. "You better not lay a finger on Julius," an opposing player warned one of his teammates, "or else Wendell will break your arm."

At about the time Erving received his on-court bodyguard, the Nets star was getting acquainted with a new off-court companion. A stunningly beautiful woman named Turquoise Brown began to cause a stir at every Nets home game, and eventually word got out that Erving and Brown were planning to get married. On their wedding day, a mob of Nets fans swarmed to Manhattan's Americana Hotel, where the ceremony was rumored to be taking place. When Erving found out that a crowd was gathering, he moved the wedding to another hotel. In a scene that foretold Erving's ability to keep his glitzy public persona separate from his family life, he and Brown were married by a justice of the peace, with only two friends looking on. Then the highly select wedding party dined on potato chips, pretzels, and vintage champagne.

After the wedding, Erving and the Nets set their sights on the division crown. Their winning ways since the meeting in San Diego had given them a slight late-season edge over the Kentucky Colonels, the preseason favorites to win the league championship. When the more experienced Kentucky squad started to pour it on down the stretch, winning 16 of 22, many expected the novices from New York to fold. First place was still up for grabs when the Nets traveled to Denver for their final regular season game.

Early in the game, Denver packed their defense around the basket, so Erving began coolly drilling long-range jumpers. By halftime he had hit for 23 points, and by the end of the third quarter he had 31. Still the Nets could not shake loose. Finally, with half of the fourth quarter gone and the Nets down by eight, the Doctor decided the time had come to take it to the rack.

Erving scored on each of four whirling, balletic drives and then dished to Brian Taylor for a layup to give the surging Nets the lead. He canned an off-balance 15-footer to up the lead to four, ripped down the rebound after a Denver miss, dribbled the shot clock down to 10, then flew past three Denver defenders for another acrobatic score.

Sensing the kill, Erving dove headlong after a loose ball, tying up Denver guard Al Smith. Denver controlled the jump, but Erving swatted away 6-foot-11-inch Dave Robisch's shot, dove again for the ball, and this time wrenched it free from a crowd. The Nets clinched the division as their superstar, who had scored 12 of their last 14 points, dribbled the game clock down to zero.

In the first round of the playoffs, the Nets rolled over Erving's former team, the Virginia Squires, in five games, setting up a showdown with the Kentucky Colonels, who had destroyed the Carolina Cougars in four.

Kentucky was led by the twin-tower combination of Dan Issel and Artis Gilmore, both future Hall of Famers. Gilmore, who measured 7 feet 8 inches from the soles of his feet to the rounded top of his enormous Afro, was the league's perennial leader in blocked shots and rebounds. When the man known as the A Train steamed toward the hoop, he scattered other giants of the league like tenpins. "When I dunk," Gilmore once said, elucidating his offensive philosophy, "I try to make the ball stick to the floor." Gilmore's inside dominance allowed Issel, the sweetest-shooting big man of his day, to roam the perimeter and bang home 18-footers to the tune of a 25.5-points-per-game average for the year.

The Nets appeared to have their hands full. "A lot of people figured these kids wouldn't be able to stand the pressure of the playoffs," said Kevin Loughery, "particularly on the road against a good, experienced team like Kentucky." The pressure of the playoffs, however, only served to inspire the whiz kids from New York. Playing a swarming help defense, they were able to slow Issel on the perimeter. Inside, the Whopper valiantly battled the A Train, bumping, bellying, elbowing, and bashing his ballyhooed counterpart to a virtual standstill. With the two Kentucky stars neutralized, Dr. J took care of the rest, and the Nets grabbed a 2–0 lead in the series.

In the third game, in Kentucky, Gilmore finally started to free himself from the sweaty, bear-hug defense of Paultz. With 9:27 left in the game, the Colonels held a 10-point lead. In other words, they were right where the Doctor wanted them. He started a 16–6 Nets run with a fairly routine jumper from the left baseline and ended the surge with a drive along the right baseline that brought him head-to-head with Gilmore. As broadcaster Van Vance once said, "Guys just didn't drive on Artis." Erving elevated and

During his years in the ABA, Erving's above-the-rim style revolutionized the game of basketball. Because of his immense crowd appeal, the established National Basketball Association (NBA) agreed to a merger with the upstart ABA after the 1976 season.

slammed the ball through Gilmore's immense claw of a left hand—and the hoop—to tie the game.

The game was still knotted with 17 seconds left. The Nets, with possession of the ball, called a time-out. Kevin Loughery had a notion, and he squatted down and began to draw up a play that would surprise everyone in the building, a play that would use the Doctor as a decoy. "Kevin," came a deep, calm voice from above the squatting coach, *"I'll take the last shot."*

There was silence in the huddle for a moment. "Okay, guys," said Loughery finally, "if Doc misses—" The coach went no further, for a huge hand had clamped down on his shoulder. "Kevin, I won't miss."

Dr. J got the ball near midcourt and dribbled the seconds down. With four ticks of the clock left, Erving drove toward the lane. Paultz demolished Erving's defender with a pick, but as Erving took off, Gilmore arrived to block his path to the basket. The Doctor veered to the right in midair and released the ball, which arced high above Gilmore's sweeping grasp.

"I can still see Julius floating to the right in the air, the shot leaving his hand," said Colonels general manager Dave Vance, "and he just ran right into the dressing room after he let it go. Julius knew it was in and he knew he had won the game."

"After Julius made that shot," said Rod Thorn, "there was no doubt in anyone's mind that we were destined to win that title." The Nets dispatched the demoralized Colonels in four games. Erving again led the way in the finals, scoring 47 of his team's 89 points in an 89–85 Game 1 squeaker over Utah. The Nets romped in Game 2 to extend their playoff winning streak to eight games.

Game 3 again proved to be the pivotal contest. In the final seconds, with the Nets down by three, the calm confidence of Dr. J pervaded the time-out huddle. "We knew something would work," said Erving. "Nobody had their heads down, praying for a hope-to-Jesus shot."

Utah, determined not to go down as Kentucky had, swarmed the Doctor on the inbounds play. They were forcing the Nets to reveal just how contagious Erving's hustle and poise could be. The ball came loose for a moment, and Wendell Ladner attacked it. As soon as he had wrestled it loose, he fired a pass to Brian Taylor, open outside the three-point line. Taylor coolly sent the game into overtime with a picture-perfect bomb. The Nets won going away.

Utah took Game 4 and then, back in New York, held a one-point lead late in Game 5. The capacity crowd at Nassau Coliseum began to make some noise as the Nets broke from a time-out huddle with 4:46 left. Williamson drilled a jump shot and the noise swelled. Paultz fired in a homely hook shot. The noise grew to a constant roar. Erving threaded the needle on a pass to Kenon and Kenon slammed. Fans were out of their seats, yelling, screaming, many of them pressing in on the edges of the court. The Doctor swished a prodigious bomb from three-point land to cap the rally, and seconds later the buzzer sent the Nets and their jubilant fans into a delirious celebration.

The precocious team from New York finally got to act their age in the locker room, pulling the old junior high school stunt of tossing the coach in the shower. A drenched Kevin Loughery lit up a victory cigar and said, "I wouldn't want it any other way. You don't get a chance to act like this too many times in your life."

"Beautiful," said Dr. J, his Afro glistening with drops of champagne. "This is the greatest thing that could happen in our first year."

During the 1974–75 season, a mixture of jealousy, complacency, and injuries crippled the Nets' drive

En route to a 47-point evening, Erving tries a scoop shot against the Utah Stars during the 1974 ABA playoffs. Averaging 27.4 points a game during the post-season, Erving led the Nets to the ABA title and was named the league's most valuable player.

Erving battles for a rebound during the 1976 playoff final against the Denver Nuggets. The Nets prevailed to win their second ABA championship, and Erving garnered his third consecutive MVP Award.

to repeat as champions. Despite improving upon their regular season record of the previous year, the young team revealed that they were prone to stretches of uninspired, selfish play. Late in the season, after struggling at home to beat a weak St. Louis Spirits team, Brian Taylor admitted, "We have to be concerned."

The Spirits, back in town for the first round of the playoffs, were described by ABA veteran Steve Jones as "talent completely out of control." Jones offered as an example the time when playground legend Fly Williams turned a routine breakaway into a 360-degree layup in which he "nearly spun himself into the floor and threw the ball right over the rim and the backboard."

The Spirits were led by a wildly erratic forward named Marvin "Bad News" Barnes. Barnes could roll out of bed and score 40 points. The tough part for Bad News was rolling out of bed. Once, as legend has it, Barnes, having missed the flight for a road game, burst into the locker room just before game time. Dressed in a floor-length fur coat and a wide-brimmed hat, he proclaimed, "Have no fear, Marvin is here." After whipping off the fur coat to reveal nothing underneath but his Spirits uniform, he went out and scored 43 points, grabbed 19 rebounds, and during a time-out, wrote a check to the charter pilot who had rushed him to the game.

Unfortunately for the Nets, the volatile mix of players from St. Louis finished the regular season on a roll. As Barnes said, "We came into these playoffs starving." The Nets managed to stave off disaster in the opener. Game 2 was a different story.

Julius Erving scored only six points. Wendell Ladner hurled his shoe at a Spirit who had stolen the ball from him. Loughery got thrown out for arguing calls; on his way out he instructed assistant coach Rod Thorn to do the same, and Thorn complied with obscene gusto.

The Nets might just as well have followed their coaches. They stumbled to defeat in Games 2, 3, and 4 and found themselves on the brink of elimination. Dr. J, who had battled back with consecutive 30-point nights, was at the center of the collapse in a fateful Game 5. His traveling violation ended the last Nets possession of the year. After helplessly watching Spirits guard Freddie Lewis drill a series-winning 20-footer at the buzzer, Erving said, "We've been confused all year. So this is how it ends: a basket in the last few seconds to end our confusion."

A sense of urgency underscored the Nets campaign in 1975–76. The ABA, after nine years, was falling apart. Players realized that a merger with the NBA might only include the best teams. The playground credo of "win or get lost" took on grim connotations as players realized their livelihood was at stake. Everyone was hungry, but no one was hungrier than Dr. J. "Julius had a gut feeling that this was the last year for the ABA," said Rod Thorn, "and he was determined to go out a champion."

Erving realized that he would have to practically do it alone. Many players who had made the 1974 championship team an ensemble effort were gone. Paultz, Kenon, and Gale had all been traded, and Wendell Ladner had met a tragic end in a plane crash. Erving took up the slack, topping the league in scoring once again and finishing in the top 10 in rebounds, assists, blocks, steals, minutes played, free-throw percentage, total field-goal percentage, and three-point field-goal percentage. Long time pro coach Alex Hannum concluded, "Julius was one of the few guys in basketball history who really could be a one-man team."

Aside from the decent backcourt work turned in by Williamson and Taylor, Erving received little support. His frontcourt help was a four-man behemoth that used its cumulative weight of 895 pounds to bludgeon playoff opponents with 224 fouls, an average of four fouls per man per game. An ugly, fight-marred semifinal series with San Antonio went to seven games before Dr. J dunked the Spurs with a last-second slam that felt to him "like a shot of life."

"When we got to the finals against Denver," said Erving, "most people figured we didn't have a chance. We hadn't won a game in Denver all season and they had the home-court advantage." Denver, the regular season champs, were led by old Nets foe Dan Issel, defensive whiz Bobby Jones, and David "Skywalker" Thompson, who in his rookie year had established himself as one of the two most spectacular players on the face of the earth. Thompson roared into the finals, eager to prove he was second to none. "He came in here like a young gunslinger after me," said Julius Erving.

But the Doctor was quicker on the draw. He made a mockery of Jones's vaunted defense, sending him to the bench with five fouls and then causing his replacement, Gus Gerard, to foul out. Erving, who finished with 45 points, 12 rebounds, and 4 assists, poured in 18 of his team's final 22 points, including the winning 18-footer over Jones as time expired.

He torched Jones in the next game for 48 points, 14 rebounds, and 8 assists, but Denver managed to salvage a win on their home floor. When Erving went to the bench with his fifth foul late in Game 3, Denver seemed poised to grab the series lead. The overmatched Nets managed to keep the score close until Erving's return with two minutes left in the fourth quarter.

The Doctor buried a pull-up jumper; head-faked Jones and drove the lane for a reverse left-handed layup; broke up a Denver two-on-one fast break by swatting Chuck Williams's shot into the stands; blocked another shot by Jones ("You don't even see him, he comes out of nowhere," reported the shell-shocked Jones); sank two free throws to seal the win; and punctuated it all with a double-pumping two-handed slam.

"I feel like I can do just about anything I want to do," Erving said. The Nets rolled in Game 4 as Erving amassed 34 points, 15 rebounds, 6 assists, 2 steals, and a blocked shot. A similar effort in Denver could not avert a loss, however, and the series returned to New York. Thompson, held by the Nets under his season average all series long, finally started to get loose in Game 6. With five minutes left in the third, Skywalker was well along in what would turn out to be a 42-point night, and the Nuggets had a commanding 80–58 lead.

Erving relaxes with his children, Cheo (left) and Julius junior, after learning of the ABA-NBA merger. Erving soon informed the Nets that he expected a new contract, one that would reward him for his role in propelling the ABA into the world of big-time sports.

Loughery called a time-out to allow his reeling players to catch their breath. For once the voluble coach chose to say nothing. As the time-out ended, he took Erving aside. "Thompson's killing us," he said. "Go get him."

Erving shut the Denver rookie down, and the Nets started to inch back into the game. The full house at Nassau Coliseum started to rock. Steve Albert, the Nets broadcaster, later recalled that the crowd "was the loudest crowd I've ever heard. They sensed that when the Nets were down by twenty, they could come back and win. They screamed and screamed and the whole thing snowballed." When Loughery saw the first flickerings of doubt on the faces of the visitors, he shouted one word to his own team: "Yellow!" This was the code word for a swarming, trapping, full-court press.

Erving was everywhere, swiping passes and attacking the boards. While he racked up nine rebounds and five steals in the fourth quarter alone, Super John Williamson started scoring at will. It was Williamson's jumper from the corner that gave the Nets the lead for good. They swept past the Nuggets to win 112–106, clinching the championship and ending the Doctor's series-long effort, which *Sports Illustrated* called "the greatest individual performance by a basketball player at any level anywhere."

In the locker room of the vanquished Nuggets, Bobby Jones muttered, "He destroys that adage that I've always been taught—that one man can't do it alone." Erving's show in the final series—he averaged 37.7 points, 14.2 rebounds, and 6 assists per game—prompted Kevin Loughery to utter, "He was just ungodly."

As rampaging Net fans stormed the court, ripping up broadcasting equipment, trashing police barricades, and hanging from the rims until the glass backboards shattered, Erving and his teammates received the trophy for the last championship of the ABA. Evidence of the league's general decay was shown in the fact that the commissioner's office could not even produce a new trophy, instead handing the champions the same piece of hardware they had won in 1974. ❖

6

A MARKED MAN

·◆·

JULIUS ERVING ENTERED the NBA smiling. Even as he was having lunch with a man who, as soon as the season began, would be trying to separate the Doctor's head from his body, Erving was unsinkably upbeat. "This is so long overdue," Erving said to his redheaded lunch companion. "It's a great, great feeling."

Dave Cowens nodded. The burly center for the Boston Celtics, like Erving, thrived at the highest level of competition. With the ABA-NBA merger finalized, the coming season promised to raise the level of play in professional basketball to unprecedented heights. Cowens said, "Now the best in the world are in one league."

During much of the meeting between the two stars, Erving celebrated the fact that many of his ABA cohorts were finally going to get a chance to step from the shadows into the limelight. "People know me," Erving said, "but there are some players who the public never heard of who can really do it."

Cowens listened as Erving listed off names of future NBA stars like George Gervin, Moses Malone, and David Thompson. Then he reeled off some names of his own. "There are a couple of tough customers waiting for you," he said. He told the Doctor of menacing enforcers like Paul Silas and Leonard Gray, and artless goons like Phil Jackson. The big man, after casually adding that "nobody's more physical than me," concluded with a friendly warning. "You must know you're a marked man in this league, Doc."

Erving accepts the congratulations of Commissioner Larry O'Brien as he holds his MVP Award after the league's 1977 All-Star Game.

Erving, aware of the NBA's bruising style, was prepared to take his licks on the court. His entry into the NBA was not going to be a smooth ride. Sometimes, Erving found out, the blows come from off the court as well.

The owner of the Nets, Raymond Boe, had promised to renegotiate Erving's contract in the event of an ABA-NBA merger, which would inevitably raise the value of the ABA franchises by a considerable amount. More than just a franchise player, the Doctor was also the single most important factor in getting the NBA owners to agree to the deal. They realized that they needed the world's most spectacular player in their league. When the merger came, however, Boe denied Erving his fair share of the spoils.

After Boe reneged on his promise, Erving decided that he had no choice but to hold out for a new contract. Erving, who had so many times broken the mold as a player on the court, began to set a new standard off the court as well. Most players before him took what they were given. Erving knew he deserved a bigger slice of the pie, and he resented the hypocrisy involved in player-management dealings.

"In the end, I sat down with Mr. Boe, and he raised the question of team loyalty," he explained. "I asked him if he could count how many players were left when we won the championship in 1974. Just two—me and Supe [John Williamson]. All the rest were traded or cut. You've got to protect yourself."

Erving found out that challenging the status quo is never easy. He was portrayed in some corners as selfish, and his spotless public image was soiled for the first time. Near the end of the long battle with Boe, Erving admitted, "I feel tarnished."

When Boe steadfastly refused to give in, Erving gave up on his desire to finish his basketball career with the Nets. Boe, in turn, gave up on Erving. "John Q. Cash does it again," noted Erving as Boe sold him down the New Jersey Turnpike to the Philadelphia 76ers.

Until this point, professional basketball for Julius Erving had still been mainly a joyous game. It was what he did best; it was the way he expressed himself. He had always been aware of the financial side of it, but his status as a mere commodity in the eyes of the owners had never before been brought home so hard. "I learned about this business," Erving said. Rich Jones, the Nets center, echoed Erving's grim awakening when he bitterly concluded, "It's a damn beef market." Kevin Loughery could only say, "Get me to a bar. I may have to become a drinkster."

As Loughery slouched off to cry in his beer, the streets of Philadelphia were peppered by a veritable hailstorm of flying champagne caps. The city's basketball fans rejoiced at the prospect of the Doctor joining what was already a powerful 76ers team. The year before, the 76ers had challenged the eventual league champions, the Celtics, for the division title and had already added a shot-blocking center from the ABA named Caldwell Jones.

Jones, when he heard Erving was following him to Philadelphia, fell to his knees and wept with joy. Doug Collins, the Sixers' slick shooting guard, stayed awake all night staring at the ceiling and laughing. George McGinnis, who in 1975 had shared the ABA Most Valuable Player (MVP) Award with Erving, exclaimed, "Me and the Doctor together? Oh my God!"

Erving, though saddened by his departure from New York, was also caught up in the rocketing expectations for Philadelphia's team. He phoned his old ABA comrade McGinnis and said, "Big George, we gonna do a number."

The potential all-pro triumvirate of Collins, Erving, and McGinnis, plus a slew of other explosive players, had the entire basketball world talking. None talked louder or with more bombast than Pat

Williams the 76ers' exuberant general manager. He said, "Would I be going too far to call this the most exciting, breathtaking team in the history of sports in this country?"

The vast fog of hype that engulfed the Sixers as they began the season masked some quiet but portentous notes of discord. "When we heard Doc was coming," one Sixer said, "there were some mixed feelings. Sure, we knew he'd be a winner, but there were also guys on this team who can play, who knew they'd be sitting when he came." McGinnis, perhaps resenting the fact that his status as the team's star player was being eclipsed, was heard to mutter, "I always felt I never got my due in the ABA. It was always Julius's league."

Pat Williams had thrown the 76ers together like a kid with a $20 bill attacking a candy rack. As if Collins, McGinnis, and Erving were not enough, the 76ers also had the talents of Lloyd B. Free at their disposal. Free, who preferred to be addressed as either All-World or The Prince of Midair, was nearly as spectacular as he thought he was. "My teammates know when there's a game to be won I'll win it for 'em," he proclaimed. "You can't stop me. You try to cut off my driving, I'll jump on you. If you jump on me, I'll jump *over* you."

Free's rival as poet laureate of the team was a teenage colossus named Darryl Dawkins, otherwise known as Double D and Chocolate Thunder. Dawkins, who had jumped straight from high school to the pros, was a 6-foot-11-inch, 265-pound 19-year-old who specialized in gaudy jewelry, extraterrestrial mythology (he claimed to be Zandokan the Mad Dunker from the distant planet Lovetron), and the demolition of backboards. He named his glass-shattering dunk against journeyman center Bill Robinzine the "Chocolate Thunder Flying, Robinzine Crying, Teeth Shaking, Glass Breaking, Rump Roasting, Bun Toasting, Wham Bam, Glass Breaker I Am Jam."

The Sixers also had the cantankerous substitute forward duo of Joe "Jellybean" Bryant and Steve Mix. Bryant, yet another one-on-one specialist, said of his rival for playing time, "Any given day I'll beat Steve's face in in any aspect of the game." Mix, who differed from other NBA hatchet men in that he, like any Sixer, loved to shoot the rock, replied, "Can you believe the head cases on this team?"

It did not take long for Erving to discover that the Sixers, for all their high-priced talent, were on course to run into some major difficulties: "The situation was created on day one in Philly that I would not play my game. I mean here I was that very first week playing tough and going all out, playing *my game* when [Sixers guard] Fred Carter said, 'Hey, easy man, you're working too hard.' Then I found out what he meant. In Philly when a man got hot and, you know, made three or four in a row, the defense didn't have to adjust to stop him because our own offense made an adjustment to stop him. *By not giving him the ball.* When it was your time, you had to do it even if you were swarmed under. You did it because you knew you wouldn't see the ball again."

The atomized collection of one-on-one stylists brought the playground to NBA arenas. Fans at home and on the road loved it, making the 76ers the most-watched team in the league. The volatile prospects for every game were impossible for a basketball fan to resist. The 76ers could fly, and they could also crash and burn.

Most damaging to their prospect of ever coming together as a team was the Sixers' ability to sustain long stretches of selfish, uninspired play and still win. By midseason, they were already virtually assured the regular season title in the weak Atlantic Division. But perceptive observers sensed that things were not going well. Erving noted, "We still have no identity. We aren't ready to make the physical, mental, and spiritual sacrifices for each other. Collectively, we are too often inept and confused."

Darryl Dawkins, also known as Zandokan the Mad Dunker, exemplified the gifted, erratic Philadelphia 76ers squad that Erving joined in 1976. Providing a steadying influence while he pumped in more than 20 points a game, Erving helped the Sixers to reach the NBA finals in his first year with the team.

One player anonymously groused, "What we got here is a bunch of babies who don't look where the real trouble is—in the mirror." The millionaires' club that was the Philadelphia 76ers refused to undergo the type of hard introspection that had brought Erving and his Nets teammates a championship in 1974. According to Doug Collins, "When we need a big basket or a key play, we fall apart." Lloyd B. Free got even deeper to the heart of the matter when he described the pressure-filled final moments of a Sixers game as "the time when we start hating each other."

Erving enjoyed a respite from the malignant atmosphere when he went to the NBA's 1977 All-Star Game. With the Sixers, he had been muting his explosive style in an attempt to mesh with his teammates. At the All-Star Game, he finally showed the NBA fans the real Doctor, skying against the best in the world for 30 spectacular points and capturing the MVP Award for the game. The experience reminded him of happier times in the ABA. It was also, for Erving, sweet vindication for all the times he and his ABA cohorts had to hear NBA men call the ABA a "minor league."

"I remember being at the first All-Star Game after the merger," Erving said, "looking around and seeing that 10 of the 24 players had been in the ABA. I said, 'Just looking at the people here, I guess that should answer any questions you have about the parity between the NBA and the ABA.'"

For Erving, the ABA had had many things that the NBA, and especially the Sixers, lacked. There had been a sense of camaraderie among all the players in the league. No one complained about long road trips punctuated by grueling red-eye flights in coach class. "They just scrunched their big bodies into those coach seats and made the best of it," said ex-coach Tom Meschery, "because they wanted to play."

In the NBA at that time, playing ball was often low on many players' lists of priorities, and the

animosity felt among Sixers teammates was actually a leaguewide phenomenon. "We aren't unique," said Sixers trainer Al Demonico, "everybody hates everybody else on every team in the league."

The 76ers paraded into the 1977 playoffs with several glaring problems. They played little defense, did not hustle back when the opposition was fast-breaking, did not pass the ball well, and did not box out well on the defensive boards. Their coach, Gene

Dr. J slams down 2 of his 30 points during his first NBA All-Star Game, played in Milwaukee, Wisconsin, on February 13, 1977. Fans who had not followed the ABA often wondered if Erving had been overhyped; his performance in Milwaukee served notice that the Doctor was for real.

Shue, was ineffectual. His apathetic approach to discipline and communication—"Players being unhappy doesn't make me unhappy. A player can say what he wants, I don't give a damn"—was in direct contrast to the type of coaching Erving had experienced with Kevin Loughery on the Nets.

But the single most unsettling problem on the team was Dr. J's passivity on the court. He had wanted to "involve others in the flow." This attempt at teamwork, however, only served to take him out of the thick of the action. Doug Collins knew that for the team to win, Erving had to become more aggressive. "We must have Doc to lead," he insisted. "Then we must learn to follow."

In the opening rounds of the playoffs, the Sixers struggled past the Boston Celtics in seven games and then disposed of the upstart Houston Rockets in six to reach the NBA finals. To that point, they had been winning as they always did, on sheer talent. With all-star center Bill Walton and his Portland Trailblazers looming, Erving finally started to take Collins's suggestion to heart. He stepped into basketball's brightest spotlight as the Dr. J of old.

Game 1 of the final kicked in with a swooping Dr. J slam off the opening tap. All game long, Erving took the ball hard to the hoop, undaunted by the presence of the towering Walton, the NBA's best shot blocker. "I'll challenge anybody," said Erving after leading the Sixers to victory with 33 points. Game 2, a 76ers romp, showed that not only was the Doctor taking the lead; his trigger-happy teammates were finally learning how to follow.

An incident occurred near the close of Game 2, however, that subtly turned the series in Portland's direction. At that point, the frustrated Trailblazers were turning the final minutes into a shoving match. McGinnis almost came to blows with Blazers bully

Lloyd Neal, and Erving's expansive cool was taxed by a barrage of elbows from enforcer Maurice Lucas. When Bobby Gross, a Portland forward, collided with Dawkins and hit the floor hard, he got up spewing curse words and threatened the Sixers manchild with a whipping.

Dawkins clenched his hands into boulder-sized fists. "Here's your chance, suckah!" he announced. Dawkins swung wildly, popping Doug Collins by mistake. Then Lucas chopped the big man in the neck from behind. Dawkins stumbled and crashed to the hardwood. A melee ensued. Both benches emptied, and fans stormed the court. Dawkins rose and started tossing bodies around like rag dolls.

Erving takes a seat on the hardwood as security personnel clear the court after a wild donnybrook during the 1977 NBA finals. When order was restored, the 76ers went on to defeat the Portland Trailblazers, 107–89.

Portland coaches traded haymakers with hooligans from the cheap seats, and Lucas fearlessly bulled through the crowd toward Dawkins, intent on finishing what he had started.

Dawkins, dragged off the court by the refs, attacked the home locker room with unbridled fury, caving in a toilet stall, flipping over two floor-to-ceiling lockers, and reducing a huge electric fan to scrap metal. "Like a hurricane had hit a junkyard," is how McGinnis described the aftermath.

The effects of the imbroglio were felt in Game 3 when an inspired Maurice Lucas laid claim to the all-important area around the basket known as the paint, scoring 27 points and ripping down 12 rebounds. The Blazers whipped the Sixers by 22. Dawkins, his passion spent, played like a timid cipher, and no one else stepped up to battle Portland's physical frontcourt.

The Blazers poured it on in the next game, winning by 32, then grabbed the series lead in Philly by pushing the Sixers around in their own building. As the Blazers forged ahead, it became apparent that they were everything the Sixers were not. A hustling, fast-breaking team, they often spun a web of laser-sharp passes in quest of an open shot. At the center of Portland's unselfish and lethal attack was Bill Walton. The big redhead blocked shots, cleared the boards, triggered the fast break, ran the floor, fired spectacular passes from the pivot, and scored when his team needed it most. "He's an inspiraton," said an admiring Erving.

On the Sixers side, no one but Erving could be described in such terms. The practices before the games in Portland had been total farces. McGinnis, mired in a monumental 16-for-48 shooting slump ("I feel like a blind man searching for the men's room"), lounged in the stands, chugging soda and chain-smoking. Dawkins, dressed in sweatpants and gaudy suspenders, shadowboxed and recited poetry: "I love

Erving battles Portland's Bill Walton for a rebound during the 1977 NBA finals. Though Erving inspired his teammates with 33 points in one game and 40 in another, the Trailblazers captured the NBA crown in six games.

fast cars and cool summer breezes, love when I want and quit when I pleases." Lloyd Free performed Harlem Globetrotter tricks, and Caldwell Jones spoke candidly with the media. "I'm missing my cartoons," Jones said. "I'll be glad when basketball is over so I can get back to my 'toons." Gene Shue finally closed his practices to the public, admitting that he made the move "out of embarrassment."

Erving went into Portland's Memorial Coliseum for Game 6 a man alone. He had taken the lead, but nobody had followed. Now it was up to him to single-handedly defeat a Blazers team on the roll of its life. He almost did. His 40 points in the teeth of a defense keying to stop him gave the Sixers a chance to tie with seconds left, but their last-ditch shots banged hard off the iron, and time ran out. The Doctor had to forge through the jubilant Portland fans who mobbed the court.

During the 1977–78 season, the 76ers picked up where they had left off in the playoffs. McGinnis was renamed "McGOONis" by Sixers fans. Shue was given the boot. Even the Doctor came under fire. Grumblings about how his best years were behind him were heard throughout the league. His statistics were down from his ABA years, and perhaps even more troubling, his midair artistry seemed a thing of the past. "The Doc can't fly no more," lamented his first pro coach, Al Bianchi.

Erving admitted, "The wear and tear has taken its toll."

Though he experienced chronic knee trouble, he attributed his fall back to earth to something other than a physical malady. "The total vibes aren't there anymore. For no reason at all, sometimes I become a passive player."

Erving had always thought of himself as a creator on the court, an artist. Now his artistic inspiration was waning. The games came and went, unmemorable and dull. The endless string of cities he traveled to whirled past him like the lights of a distant carnival ride. "I felt completely alone at times. Often, after a game and a late dinner, in one of those cities, I'd be sitting up, three o'clock, after eating a big steak, just watching that TV, with all the phones turned off." Erving heard himself asking, "Why am I different? Why, with all these great players around, guys who play as hard as I do, guys who want to win as badly as I do, why am I Dr. J?"

Deep into the long nights, the television stations would sign off. The quiet hiss of static would wash into the room. "I felt totally hollow," Erving said. The unanswered questions multiplied: "I started off asking, 'Who is Dr. J? How did I get to be him? What does being Dr. J mean?' . . . Then it came down to asking, 'Who, really, am I?' I became very frightened when I began to sense that I really had no idea."

In the summer of 1978, after another 76ers collapse in the playoffs, Erving took a trip to South Carolina for a family reunion. He was not in the best of spirits. "I had just finished a bad season," he recalled. "I had played most of it with a groin injury, my knees were bothering me, people were saying that I was over the hill as a player and the Philadelphia fans were angry. I was feeling a little sorry for myself, but when I got down there and saw all those people, people I didn't know, some of whom I didn't know existed, yet people who were connected to me in some way, it was really something. There were people I didn't even know who really cared about me and made me more aware of my family history. Because I was well known, all the people, some of whom didn't know each other, they sort of used me as a lightning rod, like a common denominator. They got closer through me. And I felt all that love passing through me. It was a very strange and wonderful feeling."

Basking in the warm South Carolina sun, centering the vast family reunion, Erving felt the troubles lift from his back. He found that nothing is sweeter than familial love, not fame, not glory, not a championship ring. "My Uncle Alphonso really simplified it for me," Erving recalled. "He said, 'Somebody along the line really laid a blessing on you.' It was as if maybe my grandmother or great-grandmother said, 'Two generations from now the first son of a second son shall be blessed.'"

Until that point, Erving said, "Everything that had occurred in my life had been a mystery to me." The good along with the bad—the soaring dunks, Marvin's death, the MVP years, the Philly fiascos— had all been equally baffling. When Erving traced the things that happened back to what made him what he was, he said, "the mysteries became clear." Erving began to sense something more powerful at work than mere flesh and bone. The vision he experienced in South Carolina led him to believe more fully in a transcendent, all-powerful love. He could feel it inside him, daring him to once again take to the sky.

7

"DARE TO BE GREAT"

WHILE JULIUS ERVING was coming alive at his family reunion, the 76ers management was experiencing an awakening of its own. Two hugely disappointing seasons caused them to take a long, hard look at their roster. They realized that throwing together a pack of superstars had not worked. They would have to pick one of the stars and build the team around him. The choice of whom to keep was easy.

"He has a presence about him," Pat Williams said of Erving. "A quiet dignity. He leads by hard work. In the past, Julius, McGinnis, and Free all wanted to be the main man. But you only have one main man on a basketball team, and we knew who it had to be."

Billy Cunningham, who had taken over for Gene Shue as the team's coach, agreed with Williams: "Julius is one of the most level-headed players I have ever known. He understands himself and he understands his teammates. I can think of no one I'd rather build a team around."

Erving, usually not one to show his emotions, was visibly moved by this vote of confidence. "He never called me about any of the honors he won before," said Turquoise Erving, "but when Billy told him he was captain, he called from practice to tell me." Julius sensed that he was entering a new phase in his career. "It's going to be a lot more challenging," he said, "and I'm ready to accept the challenge."

The Sixers began what Williams referred to as a "cleansing" by shipping Lloyd Free to San Diego, where he finally got a chance to completely spread his wings. In the coming years, he would score

Facing his former team in the 1979 playoffs, Erving puts a move on George Johnson. The Sixers, then in a rebuilding phase, got past the Nets in the opening round but then quickly faded, despite Erving's 25.4 playoff average.

89

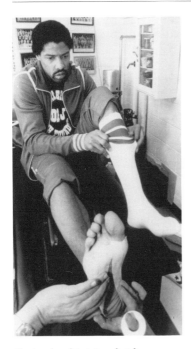

Erving has his injured right foot taped before a 1980 game against the Atlanta Hawks. Throughout his career, Erving was a remarkably durable player, missing only a handful of games over 16 seasons.

thousands of points, lose hundreds of games, and legally change his name to World B. Free.

George McGinnis was traded to Denver for Bobby Jones. This trade truly signified that the 76ers were serious about building a real team. On paper, the trade looked bad, but Jones, unlike McGinnis, was no paper tiger. The consummate role player, Jones would be helping the Sixers win long after McGinnis had ballooned in weight and hobbled off into the sunset. Jones was the defensive presence the team had lacked, as well as being an explosive finisher on the break, a fine passer, and a tenacious rebounder on the offensive glass. He stepped nicely into McGinnis's vacant forward slot, while a sleek rookie guard named Maurice Cheeks took Free's minutes as the first man off the bench. Cheeks showed the promise of things to come by leading the team in assists and steals.

The Sixers were not transformed overnight. In fact, in their first season with Erving as captain, 1978–79, they fell into second place in the Atlantic Division and bowed out quietly in the playoffs.

The next year, the NBA experienced the much-ballyhooed debut of both Larry Bird and Magic Johnson. The rapidly improving 76ers, however, almost stole the show. Erving had his best NBA year yet, finishing 4th in scoring, 7th in steals, and 10th in blocked shots. It was as if the veteran had suddenly discovered the fountain of youth. "I haven't felt so good physically or mentally since my rookie year," he said.

Though he might have felt like the high-flying 20-year-old he once was, his game had altered with the years. "Julius is getting points more quietly than he did in the ABA," said Bobby Jones. "You used to just stop and watch him. Now he just goes and goes and you hardly notice him. When he scored 44 I thought it was more like 20."

Erving himself said, "For a long time I didn't think there was anything I couldn't do on a basketball court, and I can't believe there is anything I can't do now. Only thing is, I used to be able to do them at the drop of a hat. Now I need to collect myself a little bit first."

Lesser players are unable to adapt their style as they get older. Erving, a cerebral player since he was nine years old and watching the games at Campbell Park, learned how to more fully use his wits to remain dominant into a new decade. "When players get better, when they move from one level to the next, it's not because they run faster, jump higher, or shoot straighter," he explained. "It's because they learn the game and apply what they've learned."

As the rejuvenated Dr. J led the Sixers to their best record in 12 years, two other supreme students of the game were also leading their respective teams to the top. Larry Bird captured rookie of the year honors in 1980 as his Celtics rolled to 61 victories and the Atlantic Division crown. Out west, Magic Johnson teamed with Kareem Abdul-Jabbar to make the Los Angeles Lakers the odds-on favorite for the league title.

Erving and the Sixers upset Bird's Celtics in the playoffs before falling prey to not one but two of the most impressive championship-round performances of all time. First, Abdul-Jabbar dominated the Philadelphia big men in leading the Lakers to a three-games-to-two advantage. Prospects brightened for the Sixers when an injury forced Abdul-Jabbar to the sidelines for Game 6, but at that point Magic Johnson announced to the world, once and for all, that he had arrived. Playing every position on the floor, including the pivot, the 6-foot-9-inch wizard erupted for 42 points, 15 rebounds, 7 assists, and 3 steals. All Dr. J could muster as he sat in the quiet locker room after the game was a shake of the head and one word: "Unreal."

As the following season unfolded, it became apparent that there was more than one pro basket-

Erving makes Kareem Abdul-Jabbar pay the price as the Lakers center jams during the 1980 NBA finals. Erving had led the Sixers to their best regular-season record in 12 years, but they fell short in the playoffs once again, thanks to a 42-point effort in Game 6 by rookie Magic Johnson.

ball league. In addition to the NBA, there was an unnamed, highly exclusive league that included only the Celtics, the Lakers, and the 76ers. Over the next six years, this unapproachable triumvirate would supply 10 of the 12 playoff finalist teams. No team from outside this group would win the NBA championship in that span of time.

At first glance, it appeared that the Sixers might be the weakest of the three dominant teams. Celtics president Red Auerbach shrewdly surrounded Larry Bird with future Hall of Famers like Robert Parish, Kevin McHale, Tiny Archibald, and a bit later, Dennis Johnson. Lakers owner Jerry Buss, meanwhile, spared no expense in creating a similarly luminous supporting cast for Magic and Kareem, outfitting stars like Jamaal Wilkes, Norm Nixon, James Worthy, A. C. Green, Byron Scott, Michael Cooper, and Bob McAdoo in the Lakers purple and gold.

The Sixers could not match their rivals in the number of marquee players. But they stayed competitive on the strength of their number one star and a host of decent role players. Up front was the so-called gruesome twosome of Caldwell Jones and Darryl Dawkins. Dawkins began to show more and more flashes of his seemingly unlimited potential. Occasionally, Zandokan the Mad Dunker looked like the best center on the planet Earth, running the floor, rebounding, draining smooth jumpers from the top of the key, and blasting to the hole for raucous dunks. Whenever he pulled his disappearing act and returned to the mysterious planet Lovetron, the ever-consistent Caldwell Jones was there to pick up the slack.

In the backcourt, the Sixers featured the three-guard attack of Maurice Cheeks, Lionel Hollins, and Andrew Toney. Cheeks quickly developed into the prototypical NBA point guard. When the Sixers had the ball, he ran the offense with precision and style and never took a bad shot. When the opposition was on the attack, the bullet-quick guard, who would retire as the all-time NBA leader in steals, was the best of his time at getting the ball back. Hollins, another fine defensive player, was the most versatile of the threesome. He could heat up at the shooting guard position or run the team when Cheeks went to the bench. Toney, who started getting minutes when the oft-injured Doug Collins finally hung it up in 1980–81, checked into the game when the Sixers needed a burst of adrenaline. Reminiscent of the man named Free, Toney could score from anywhere.

Bobby Jones, Steve Mix, and jumping-jack guard Clint Richardson rounded out the team. Billy Cunningham directed the cohesive, defense-oriented attack from the sidelines, watching as his hustling acrobats turned steals and blocked shots into easy fast-break scores. When the game clock ticked down to the final seconds, the new, improved Sixers knew what to do. They looked to their main man and got out of the way.

The man the Sixers counted on was, in the early 1980s, the best player in basketball. Dr. J topped an excellent campaign in 1979–80 by becoming the league MVP in 1980–81. He led the Sixers in scoring and blocks and was second in rebounds, assists, and steals. On a grander scale, Erving's MVP Award, the first given to a noncenter in 17 years, symbolized a change in the way NBA basketball was played. Erving had pioneered this change by showing that the game could be dominated from the perimeter.

In the 1981 playoffs, after the Doctor outdueled Marques Johnson and the Milwaukee Bucks in seven games, the Sixers flew to Boston to take on the Celtics in what many viewed as the real league final. Out west, the Lakers had been stunned in the first round by the Houston Rockets, so it was generally considered that the winner of the East would easily march to the title.

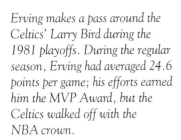

Erving makes a pass around the Celtics' Larry Bird during the 1981 playoffs. During the regular season, Erving had averaged 24.6 points per game; his efforts earned him the MVP Award, but the Celtics walked off with the NBA crown.

The Sixers stormed to a three-games-to-one advantage. The proud Celtics then rallied to stave off elimination in their own building before returning to the Spectrum for what looked to be the final game, as the Sixers were nearly unbeatable at home. Celtics rookie Kevin McHale, however, preferred to look on the bright side of his team's long Spectrum losing streak. "Everybody's been talking about a jinx," he said. "Well, what about the law of averages? Put chimps on roller skates, let them play in the Spectrum enough times and sooner or later they'll win."

Nobody would ever confuse Larry Bird's Celtics with chimps on roller skates. In Game 6, in fact, spurred by forward Cornbread Maxwell's violent foray into the hostile stands, they more closely resembled gorillas on a motorcycle rampage. As bodies flew in the paint and debris rained down from every corner of the arena, the rough men in green knotted the series at three.

Game 7 looked like more of the same as Celtics bashers McHale, Parish, and Rick Robey neutralized the Sixers running game. But midway through the fourth period, Julius Erving had brought his weary team back into the lead. He drilled a bank shot, flicked in a layup, jammed on the break, swished a long jumper, and cashed in an offensive rebound on a pretty, twisting reverse layin. With 5:23 left, Erving had pushed his team in front by six.

One year before, the 76ers had been taught a painful lesson about the newcomer known as Magic. The spring of 1981 would come to a similar close as the Sixers learned about the man Bostonians simply called Larry. In the final minutes, Bird picked off two passes in a row, outletting both times to a streaking teammate for a score, before draining a pair of free throws to tie the game at 89. Bird then blocked Erving's shot, grabbed the rebound, and dribbled the length of the floor to knock in a bank shot. After a Mo Cheeks free throw, the Sixers had a last-second chance to win, but Bobby Jones's half-court alley-oop pass bounced high off the backboard, just inches from Erving's grasp. "This is a down time," was all the Doctor could say after the game. "See you next year."

The next year looked to be a frightening repeat of the year before. The Sixers, for the third year in a row, snatched a 3–1 lead against the Celtics in the Eastern Division finals. For the second year in a row, the Celtics battled back to send the deadlocked series back to Boston for a seventh game.

"After the sixth game," recalled Clint Richardson, "practically everybody had given up on us, and we had nowhere to go but each other. It was a bad feeling and it hurt us, but it made the guys who were involved in that situation closer." Sixers fans, wounded by the collapse of 1981, practically conceded the game to Boston. History provided the grim

Erving confers with 76ers coach Billy Cunningham during a tense moment in the 1982 playoffs. Since 1976, Cunningham and General Manager Pat Williams had gradually rebuilt the Sixers around Erving's talent and leadership qualities.

fact that the Celtics were virtually unbeatable in their building in a final-game situation. To emphasize the point, Celtics rooters paraded by the Sixers bench dressed in sheets bearing the words "Ghosts of Celtics Past" along with the numbers of players from previous championship teams, such as Bill Russell, John Havlicek, and Sam Jones.

"That's when I got scared," joked Erving. "I thought it was the Klan."

Erving epitomized the paradoxically jovial mood of the Sixers as they stepped onto Boston Garden's parquet floor for the opening tap. The smiles on all the Sixers' faces were the work of Darryl Dawkins, who had been ordered by Billy Cunningham to rip off a few choice one-liners just as the game was about to begin. While Celtics coach Bill Fitch was yelling in the final pregame huddle about back-picks and the transition game, Dawkins spun an off-color rhyme about a man from Nantucket.

The Sixers just relaxed and played ball. The game, despite a modest Celtics charge in the third quarter, was never really in question. Erving dumped in 29 points; Toney, tagged by Beantown scribes as the Boston Strangler, had no trouble with his windpipe as he erupted for 34; and the Sixers won going away, 120–106. Celtics fans, impressed by the competitive fire, resiliency, and class of Dr. J's team, paid tribute with seconds left in the game by rocking the rafters with a brand-new chant: "Beat L.A.! Beat L.A.!"

The Los Angeles Lakers had torn up the West. Their consecutive four-game sweeps of Phoenix and San Antonio had left them just one game short of a share of the all-time record for most consecutive playoff victories. The Sixers, after dropping the first game to the blitzkreig from L.A., managed to stave off the ignominy of being record-breaking victims by winning the second game in the Spectrum. It was clear, however, that the Lakers were on an unstoppable roll. It seemed they had an emphatic answer to everything the Sixers tried.

Late in Game 6, Erving got loose for one of his patented scoring flurries, pouring in eight points in less than two minutes. For a moment it appeared the Sixers were going send the series back to Philadelphia for Game 7. Erving attempted to cap the burst with a soaring dunk—a play that would have given his team their first lead of the night—but old pro Bob McAdoo swooped in to block the Doctor's shot from behind. Abdul-Jabbar slammed home a deuce on the ensuing fast break, and the Lakers never looked back.

Erving's spirit was not broken. As the Forum fans hailed their champions, the Doctor, sitting by his locker, stared into the television lights. A voice from

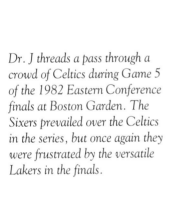

Dr. J threads a pass through a crowd of Celtics during Game 5 of the 1982 Eastern Conference finals at Boston Garden. The Sixers prevailed over the Celtics in the series, but once again they were frustrated by the versatile Lakers in the finals.

out of the white glare wanted to know if, after five years of near misses, Dr. J ever felt like giving up. "Unless you dare to put yourself at center stage," he quietly replied, "dare to be great, you never can be. I'm going to keep daring. As I dared in the past, I'll dare in the future."

No one could question Erving's determination and courage. But it was becoming painfully clear that his team was just a little bit short. On the Lakers, when Kareem was double- or triple-teamed in the paint, he could dish off to Magic. On the Celtics, Bird could lean on the clutch shooting of his front-court mates McHale and Parish. The Sixers had one option and one option only when the pressure was on. It was not enough.

In Philadelphia hopes of a championship grew even dimmer when the Lakers, after some savvy maneuvering, snared the first pick in the college draft, an explosive forward from North Carolina named James Worthy. The Sixers knew that they could not compete using the players that they had. They dumped Caldwell Jones, Lionel Hollins, Steve Mix, and Darryl Dawkins. There was one man that they had their eyes on, and he was not going to come cheaply. Using the money they saved from jettisoning the veterans, the Sixers pulled the trigger on the deal of the century. They went into the free-agent market and snagged Moses Malone. ◖◗

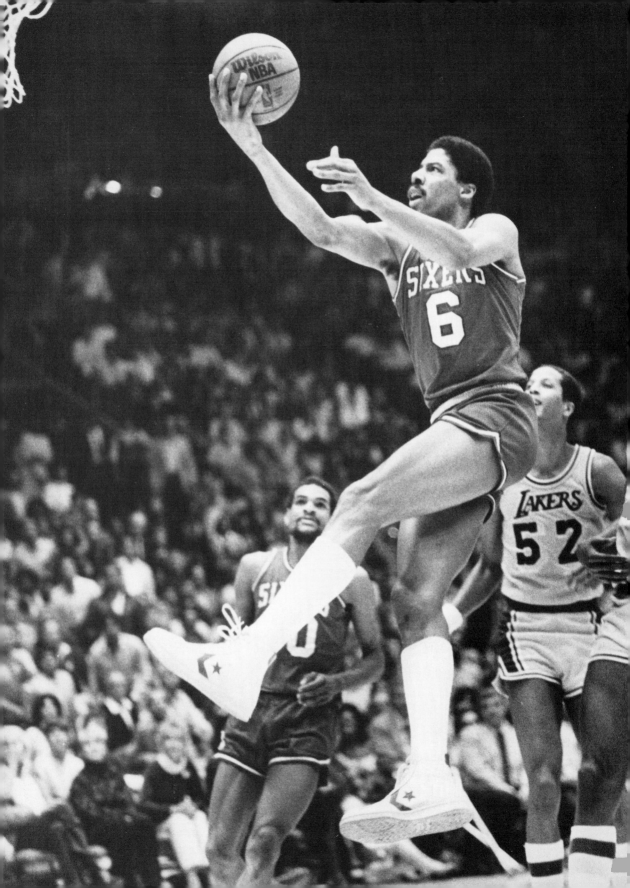

8

KNOWING HOW TO LAND

———— ❦ ————

"THERE ARE A lot of forces in nature you don't stop," Lakers forward Kurt Rambis once said, "and Moses Malone is one of them." When Malone came to the Sixers in 1982, he was at the height of his phenomenal career. The year before, he had won the MVP Award while averaging 31.1 points and 14.7 rebounds a game.

Malone did not have a pretty shot. He was not particularly fast, could not leap, and his hands were so small he may have been the only NBA player unable to palm the ball. But Moses Malone, arguably the best center in the league, dominated games by pure hustle. He used his less-than-Herculean body to get position in the low post, and from there he would pound and pound, all night long, until his defender resembled a tall strand of cooked linguine.

"We had most of the parts," Julius Erving aptly summed up, "and then we went out and paid cold cash for a hard hat." Malone's work ethic renewed the beleaguered franchise. "He works so hard," said a Sixers official, "that he makes the other players feel guilty if they don't put out as much effort."

Dr. J was one player who welcomed the more rigorous atmosphere. Erving had always prided himself on his work ethic. Ever since his first days in Philadelphia, when a teammate had told him not to work so hard, he had never felt quite right. He and Malone were actually two of a kind, despite outward appearances. Erving had always made his game look effortless, barely even breaking a sweat. But behind all the artful moves were hours and hours of hard work. "Out of one hundred moves I make," Erving

Closing in on his ultimate goal, Erving adds 2 points to Philadelphia's lead in the 1983 playoff finale against the Lakers. Moments later, the Sixers emerged with a 115–108 victory and their first NBA championship.

Sixers center Moses Malone seeks to drive around Kurt Rambis in Game 3 of the 1983 finals. By signing the intense, hardworking Malone as a free agent, the Sixers added the final ingredient they needed for a title.

once said, talking about his practice regimen. "I've made 99 before."

As he entered his 11th year in the pros, he was still constantly on the lookout for ways to improve. "Even now I'll be watching a game somewhere and I'll see somebody do something that'll remind me of something I've forgotten—some little move maybe. I'll practice it a little, and I've got it back, and when the right situation comes along, against some player, maybe I've got a little edge I didn't have before."

One of the things Erving had to work on as the 1982–83 season began was stepping down as the team's top gun. Although Malone joined the team with the self-effacing announcement, "It's Julius's team, I'm just here to work hard," it was clear to Erving that his role would have to change. "When you become the second or third option on a play, it requires some adjustments," Erving said. "Sometimes I wasn't able to make that adjustment. I'd get lost, out of my rhythm. That's when you have to step back and regroup."

As the year went on, Erving proved more than adept at being the number two man, and the Sixers, quickly outdistancing all competition, began to look like a team for the ages. Near the close of the year, they were on a pace to break the all-time record for games won in a regular season. Bobby Jones knew why: "The aggressiveness we have is consistent every night. I've never seen a team that had it like this team does. Every night our opponent knows what they're going to face for 48 minutes, and we don't let up."

The Sixers were driven by an unmatched hunger. "We haven't had the ultimate success," said Erving, "and we've got guys this year who really want it." Regular-season records meant little to the team, so after they wrapped up home-court advantage for the playoffs, they slackened the pace and fell short of the 1972 Lakers' record for wins in a season. They were saving it for the playoffs. Malone, asked by his coach how he viewed the upcoming postseason action, confidently replied, "Fo', fo', and fo'."

Malone's prediction that the Sixers would dispatch all their playoff opponents in four games hit a slight snag when the Bucks snuck a game from them in the conference finals. Still, when they entered the championship round, they had won eight out of their nine playoff games. All that remained were the tormentors from the West known as the Los Angeles Lakers.

Erving did it all in Game 1, posting a line of 20 points, 10 rebounds, 9 assists, and 5 blocked shots. The Sixers, feeding on years of frustration at the hands of Magic's team, beat the Lakers into submission. A glassy-eyed Norm Nixon admitted, "I think that we were shocked by their physicalness and their overall aggressiveness." The Sixers had carved out three workmanlike wins before the Lakers even knew what hit them. Then, in Game 4, the Lakers fast break began to click. They raced into the fourth quarter with an 11-point lead. Moses Malone refused to worry. "I could see them tightening up," he said. "They saw us comin' again, comin' again. The train was comin' again."

Malone, who tore down 10 of his 23 rebounds in the final quarter, was unquestionably the Sixers engine. But the conductor of the furious Sixers rally was none other than Dr. J. With two minutes to play and the Sixers still down by a bucket, Erving knocked the ball loose from Michael Cooper, beat the fleet swingman down the floor, grabbed the ball, and taking off from just inside the foul line, threw down a self-described "no doubt about it" dunk.

"He took over the game and put it in his back pocket," said longtime Doctor watcher Bobby Jones. Erving gave the Sixers the lead with a driving three-

Erving and Sixers guard Andrew Toney react to the cheers of a capacity crowd at Philadelphia's Veterans Stadium on June 2, 1983. Following a victory parade through downtown Philadelphia, jubilant Sixers fans jammed the Vet to celebrate their long-awaited NBA championship.

point play, and then, with the shot clock running down on the next possession, he nailed shut the Lakers coffin with a fall-away 18-footer that kissed through the bottom fringe of the twine.

"We did it the hard way, we did it the long way, but we did it better than anyone else," said Erving after the game. In another corner of the exuberant locker room, Billy Cunningham offered a similar epitaph for the team that would go down in history as one of the best ever. "We toyed with people, just toyed with them."

Moses Malone, drenched in sweat and champagne, slumped at his locker, looking tired for the first time all season, "This was for Doc," he said in a quiet voice. "I wanted to be able to say that I played on a world championship team with Dr. J."

The 76ers could not remain on top in the NBA. By 1986, ravaged by injuries, they were a mere shadow of their former selves. A player coming to the end of his career on a declining team might find cause for despair. But for Julius Erving, who had never allowed basketball to be the only thing in his life, 1986 was in many ways a good year.

First of all, he experienced the continuing joy of being with his four children, Cheo, Julius junior, Jazmin, and Cory. Erving had also savored the sense of fulfillment that came from his tireless charitable works. He was, among other things, spokesman for the Lupus Foundation, the coach for a Special Olympics program, adviser to the March of Dimes, and the national chairman of the Hemophilia Foundation.

In 1986, Erving also made gains in the business world, joining with a group of black businessmen to acquire the Philadelphia Coca-Cola Bottling Company. Philadelphia Coke became the first Coca-Cola bottling enterprise to be held by black ownership. The company ranked fourth in sales among all black-owned businesses in the United States.

Later in the year, Erving fulfilled a promise that he had made to his mother 15 years before. Clad in a mortarboard and an extralong gown, the 76ers millionaire strode across the University of Massachusetts commencement stage to receive his bachelor's degree in business. Like the purchase of Philadelphia Coke, the diploma symbolized Erving's desire to take more from life than just the spoils of athletic success. By the time he received his B.A., he had already given a lot of thought to the day he would no longer pull on his Sixers uniform.

He approached the subject of his waning athletic prowess on a spiritual level. "I believe I was given a

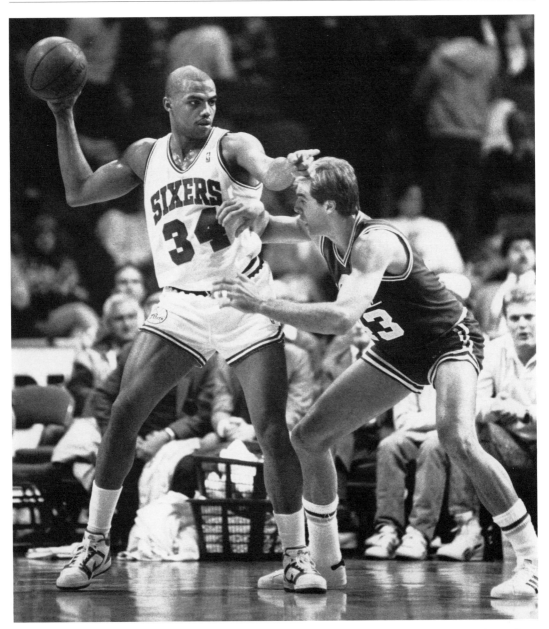

As Dr. J's brilliant career was winding down, Charles Barkley began to emerge as the 76ers' new superstar.

gift." he said, "And what can be given can be taken away." Far from growing bitter over the ephemeral nature of the gift, Erving saw that what was important was not the gift itself, but the fact that it had been given at all. Basketball had taught him, he said, that "there wasn't anything I couldn't do." He realized as the years went on that this teaching applied to more than just basketball. "That belief has been expanded to the point where I feel that *nothing* is impossible. And if nothing is impossible, then basketball is just a tiny part of it."

Erving's final years on the court were scored by an arc of graceful descent. A young Michael Jordan was easing the mantle of the most spectacular athlete in the world away from the Doctor. On Dr. J's own team, a wrecking ball called Charles Barkley was taking center stage. The veteran's once explosive game was now the model of quiet consistency.

Accolades showered down on Erving from the players who were rising up to take his place at the top of the game. Isiah Thomas, the Detroit Pistons' star guard, said, "You have been an inspiration, a leader, and a perfect role model for me and all the other NBA players. You have made the path much smoother for us younger guys to follow." Magic Johnson, in his praise, focused on what Erving was able to accomplish on the court. "The Doc changed ball. The Doc went past jumps, hooks, sets, went past everything and made the playground *official*."

Erving's last trip around the league in 1987 evoked a sometimes touching, sometimes bombastic series of official tributes. Everywhere he went, the home team was ready with long speeches and piles of booty. At the Boston Garden, Larry Bird presented the Doc with a piece of the hallowed parquet floor. Kareem Abdul-Jabbar presided as the Lakers gave the aging star a rocking chair. Among many other gifts large and small, he got skis, a pair of boots, a machine that served tennis balls, and the key to the city of Indianapolis.

The farewell tour was a chance for fans around the country to say good-bye to the player who had entertained and inspired them for so many years. For the most part, Erving kept his own emotions in check. Then he traveled up the New Jersey Turnpike to play a final game against his old team, the Nets.

Erving had once vowed, when his brother had died, that nothing would ever make him cry again. But at halftime of the Sixers-Nets game, as the red-white-and-blue Nets uniform with the name ERVING and the number 32 was being raised to the rafters, the Doctor felt something well up inside him that he could not control. On hand were his mother, his old coach from UMass, Jack Leaman, and several of his teammates from the Nets' championship teams. "I can't bear to look up there," Erving said into the microphone, a hitch in his voice. Up in the rafters, the uniform shivered as it halted in place. Erving finally looked up. The glorious days of soaring dunks and last-second wins and locker rooms flooded with laughter and champagne were in the past, and not even the Doctor could reach up and get them back.

Julius Erving was, however, good for one more day of glory. With two games to go in his final season, he needed 36 points to join Kareem Abdul-Jabbar and Wilt Chamberlain as the only three players to score 30,000 career points. Scoring from everywhere, with three-pointers, driving layups, twisting bank shots, rebound tip-ins, and of course, a bevy of vintage Dr. J dunks, Erving torched the Indiana Pacers for 38 points and reminded the sold-out Spectrum crowd that the record breaker with flecks of gray in his hair could still play some ball.

After the final jump shot was sunk, the crowds still flocked to the Doctor. Erving had never taken the adulation of fans lightly. As the father of four children, he was especially concerned with how he was being perceived by young people. "They come at me all the time, yelling, 'Hey, Doc! Hey Dr. J!' That's cool. I answer them in a minute," Erving said. "But I never encourage them to be like me. 'There are 250

pro basketball players in a country of 250 million people,' I tell them. 'You think you're one in a million? If there were a million guys lined up here, could you beat them all one-on-one?' "

Erving's graphic message was not meant to dash the dreams of anyone. He simply wanted black youths to see their situation clearly and to see that Erving's own success had not been easily won. "I want them to see I am a hard-working successful black man."

Flanked by his mother, Callie Mae, and his wife, Turquoise, Erving acknowledges the crowd during a 1987 farewell ceremony at New York's Madison Square Garden. As he prepared to retire from the game, Erving was hailed by fans and fellow players, who appreciated his character as much as his ability.

Dr. J's popularity was such in Philadelphia that he got his own parade in April 1987, shortly before playing his final NBA game. He ended his career as one of only three players to score more than 30,000 lifetime points in professional basketball.

In 1993, Julius Erving was inducted into the Basketball Hall of Fame, in Springfield, Massachusetts. "I never had any trouble jumping," Erving said to the large gathering of reporters, fans, and basketball greats. "The key to jumping is knowing how to land." This made the crowd at the induction ceremony laugh. After five smooth years of postbasketball life, Erving had come down where all basketball immortals are bound to land.

Erving told a story while he was up on the podium. It went beyond what he had been saying for years, that his success was simply a product of hard work and strong faith. These counted, to be sure, but there was always a feeling that Dr. J's greatness came from something more. There was some other spark in the mix, a daringness, a courage, a desire to live each day like the life-and-death game that it was. The story revealed that this spark had been with Erving even before he took the court for the first time.

"When I was 6 or 7 years old," he said, "I was jumping out of swings in the playground. The roll, the parachute, all of it. We had a game called Geronimo. You'd jump, yell 'Geronimo!' float and land." Erving paused and looked out over the crowd, letting the image of a soaring Julius Erving settle in everyone's mind. A boy shoots alone up into the sky, he twists, he flips, he soars. A man lands firmly on the dusty earth. "Then you'd look back at the next guy," Erving said to the rapt crowd. "You'd look back and say, 'Match that!' "

APPENDIX:
CAREER STATISTICS

REGULAR SEASON RECORD

VIRGINIA SQUIRES (VA), NEW YORK NETS (NY), PHILADELPHIA 76ERS (PHI)

YEAR	G	MIN	FGM	FGA	PCT	FTM	FTA	PCT	—REBOUNDS— OFF	DEF	TOT	AST	PTS	AVG
71-72 VA*	84	3,513	910	1,826	.498	467	627	.745	—	—	1319	335	2,290	27.3
72-73 VA*	71	2,993	894	1,804	.496	475	612	.776	—	—	867	298	2,268	31.9
73-74 NY*	84	3,398	914	1,785	.512	454	593	.766	263	639	899	434	2,299	27.4
74-75 NY*	84	3,402	914	1,806	.506	486	608	.799	284	630	914	462	2,343	27.9
75-76 NY*	84	3,244	949	1,873	.507	530	662	.801	337	588	925	423	2,462	29.3
76-77 PHI	82	2,940	685	1,373	.499	400	515	.777	192	503	695	306	1,770	21.6
77-78 PHI	74	2,429	611	1,217	.502	306	362	.845	179	302	481	279	1,528	20.6
78-79 PHI	78	2,802	715	1,455	.491	373	501	.745	198	366	564	357	1,803	23.1
79-80 PHI	78	2,812	838	1,614	.519	420	534	.787	215	361	576	355	2,100	26.9
80-81 PHI	82	2,874	794	1,524	.521	422	536	.787	244	413	657	364	2,014	24.6
81-82 PHI	81	2,789	780	1,428	.546	411	539	.763	220	337	557	319	1,974	24.4
82-83 PHI	72	2,421	605	1,170	.517	330	435	.759	173	318	491	263	1,542	21.4
83-84 PHI	77	2,683	678	1,324	.512	364	483	.754	190	342	532	309	1,727	22.4
84-85 PHI	78	2,535	610	1,236	.494	338	442	.765	172	242	414	233	1,561	20.0
85-86 PHI	74	2,474	521	1,085	.480	289	368	.785	169	201	370	248	1,340	18.1
86-87 PHI	60	1,918	400	850	.471	191	235	.813	115	149	264	191	1,005	16.8
NBA TOTALS	836	28,677	7,237	14,276	.507	3,844	4,950	.777	2,067	3,534	5,601	3,224	18,364	22.0
ABA TOTALS	407	16,550	4,581	9,094	.504	2,412	3,102	.778	—	—	4,924	1,952	11,662	28.7
NBA PLAYOFF TOTALS	141	5,288	1,187	2,441	.486	707	908	.779	360	634	994	594	3,088	21.9
ABA PLAYOFF TOTALS	48	2,064	582	1,122	.519	318	400	.795	—	—	617	247	1,492	31.1

* INDICATES ABA TEAM

CHRONOLOGY

———— ❧ ————

1950   Born Julius Winfield Erving, II in Hempstead, New York, on February 22

1961   Father dies in car accident; Erving leads his Salvation Army Youth League team to a 31-1 record

1969   Enrolls in University of Massachusetts; leads UMass freshman team to an undefeated mark; younger brother, Marvin, dies of lupus erythematosus

1970   UMass gains bid to the National Invitational Tournament (NIT); Erving leads Olympic development team in scoring and rebounding

1971   UMass Minutemen compile their best record ever; Erving becomes one of only seven Division I players to average 20 points and 20 rebounds per game in the same season; skips senior season to sign with the Virginia Squires of the American Basketball Association (ABA)

1972   Leads all ABA players in postseason scoring, rebounds, and assists

1973   Erving leads ABA in scoring with 31.9 average; sold to the New York Nets

1974   Marries Turquoise Brown; leads ABA in scoring; Nets win the ABA championship; Erving wins the ABA's Most Valuable Player Award

1975   Scores 63 points in a game against the San Diego Conquistadors; wins second straight MVP Award

1976   Wins first-ever slam dunk contest; leads ABA in scoring; Nets win the ABA championship; Erving wins third straight MVP award; ABA merges with NBA (National Basketball Association); Erving sold to the Philadelphia 76ers

1977   Wins NBA All-Star Game MVP Award; 76ers win Atlantic Conference championship and reach NBA finals

1978   Erving named to the All-NBA first team; 76ers repeat as Atlantic Conference champions; Erving named captain of the 76ers

1980   76ers reach finals after compiling their best record in 12 years

1981   Erving becomes the first noncenter in 17 years to win the NBA's Most Valuable Player Award

1983   Wins the NBA All-Star Game MVP Award; 76ers win the NBA championship; Erving wins the J. Walter Kennedy Citizenship Award

1986   Earns a bachelor's degree in business from the University of Massachusetts; joins with other black businessmen to purchase the Philadelphia Coca-Cola Bottling Company

1987   Becomes one of only three players in the history of professional basketball to score over 30,000 points; announces his retirement from basketball

1993   Elected to the Basketball Hall of Fame; joins NBC as studio analyst for NBA games

FURTHER READING

———— ❦ ————

Abdul-Jabbar, Kareem, with Mignon McCarthy. *Kareem*. New York: Warner, 1990.

Axthelm, Pete. *The City Game: Basketball from the Garden to the Playground*. New York: Penguin, 1982.

Bell, Marty. *The Legend of Doctor J*. New York: Signet, 1981.

Dolan, Sean. *Magic Johnson*. New York: Chelsea House, 1993.

George, Nelson. *Elevating the Game: The History and Aesthetics of Black Men in Basketball*. New York: Simon & Schuster, 1991.

Halberstam, David. *The Breaks of the Game*. New York: Random House, 1981.

Hollander, Zander, and Alex Sachare. *The Official NBA Basketball Encyclopedia*. New York: New American Library, 1989.

Pluto, Terry. *Loose Balls*. New York: Simon & Schuster, 1990.

Telander, Rick. *Heaven Is a Playground*. New York: Simon & Schuster, 1991.

Wielgus, Chuck, and Alexander Wolff. *The In-Your-Face Basketball Book*. New York: Wynwood, 1980.

INDEX

PICTURE CREDITS

JOSH WILKER has a degree in creative writing and literature from Johnson State College. He is the author of *The Lenape Indians* in Chelsea House's JUNIOR LIBRARY OF AMERICAN INDIANS series and is currently at work on a biography of automobile racer A. J. Foyt.

NATHAN IRVIN HUGGINS, one of America's leading scholars in the field of black studies, helped select the titles for the BLACK AMERICANS OF ACHIEVEMENT series, for which he also served as senior consulting editor. He was the W.E.B. Du Bois Professor of History and of Afro-American Studies at Harvard University and the director of the W.E.B. Du Bois Institute for Afro-American Research at Harvard. He received his doctorate from Harvard in 1962 and returned there as a professor in 1980 after teaching at Columbia University, the University of Massachusetts, Lake Forest College, and the California State University, Long Beach. He was the author of four books and dozens of articles, including *Black Odyssey: The Afro-American Ordeal in Slavery*, *The Harlem Renaissance*, and *Slave and Citizen: The Life of Frederick Douglass*, and was associated with the Children's Television Workshop, National Public Radio, the Boston Athenaeum, the Museum of Afro-American History, the Howard Thurman Educational Trust, and Upward Bound. Professor Huggins died in 1989, at the age of 62, in Cambridge, Massachusetts.